THE SIGNERS

OF

THE DECLARATION

OF

INDEPENDENCE

By Robert G. Ferris and
Richard E. Morris

Eastern National

John Penn   John Hancock   John Ha...

Floyd   Wm Pa...

Geo Read   Wm Hooper   Saml Adams

St. Hopkins   Thos Nelson jr   Geo Clymer

Charles Carroll of Carrollton   Elbridge Gerr...

Tho M:Kean   Roger Sherman   Sam Huntington

Wm Whipple   Thomas Lynch Junr.

Taylor   Josiah Bartlett   Benj Frankl...

Wm Williams   Richd Stockton

John Morto...

Oliver Wolcott   Jno Witherspoon   Geo Ro...

Tho Stone   Samuel Chase   Robt Treat Pain...

George Wythe   Matthew Thornton

Fran[s] Lewis   Th Jefferson   Benjd Harrison

Lewis Morris   Abra Clark   Phil. Livings...

Casar Rodne...

Arthr Middleton   Fras Hopkinson

Geo Walton   Carter Braxton   James Wilso...

Richard Henry Lee   Thos Heyward Junr

Benjamin Rush   John Adams   Robt Morr...

Lyman Hall   Joseph Hewes   Button Gwinne...

Francis Lightfoot Lee

William Ellery   Edward Rutledge   Jas Smith

TABLE OF CONTENTS

Fourth of July, 1875, engraving by John McRae.

In CONGRESS, July 4, 1776.

A DECLARATION

By the REPRESENTATIVES of the

UNITED STATES OF AMERICA,

In GENERAL CONGRESS ASSEMBLED.

WHEN in the Course of human Events, it becomes neceſſary for one People to diſſolve the Political Bands which have connected them with another, and to aſſume among the Powers of the Earth, the ſeparate and equal Station to which the Laws of Nature and of Nature's God entitle them, a decent Reſpect to the Opinions of Mankind requires that they ſhould declare the cauſes which impel them to the Separation.

WE hold theſe Truths to be ſelf-evident, that all Men are created equal, that they are endowed by their Creator with certain unalienable Rights, that among theſe are Life, Liberty, and the Purſuit of Happineſs--That to ſecure theſe Rights, Governments are inſtituted among Men, deriving their juſt Powers from the Conſent of the Governed, that whenever any Form of Government becomes deſtructive of theſe Ends, it is the Right of the People to alter or to aboliſh it, and to inſtitute new Government, laying its Foundation on ſuch Principles, and organizing its Powers in ſuch Form, as to them ſhall ſeem moſt likely to effect their Safety and Happineſs. Prudence, indeed, will dictate that Governments long eſtabliſhed ſhould not be changed for light and tranſient Cauſes; and accordingly all Experience hath ſhewn, that Mankind are more diſpoſed to ſuffer, while Evils are ſufferable, than to right themſelves by aboliſhing the Forms to which they are accuſtomed. But when a long Train of Abuſes and Uſurpations, purſuing invariably the ſame Object, evinces a Deſign to reduce them under abſolute Deſpotiſm, it is their Right, it is their Duty, to throw off ſuch Government, and to provide new Guards for their future Security. Such has been the patient Sufferance of theſe Colonies; and ſuch is now the Neceſſity which conſtrains them to alter their former Syſtems of Government. The Hiſtory of the preſent King of Great-Britain is a Hiſtory of repeated Injuries and Uſurpations, all having in direct Object the Eſtabliſhment of an abſolute Tyranny over theſe States. To prove this, let Facts be ſubmitted to a candid World.

HE has refuſed his Aſſent to Laws, the moſt wholeſome and neceſſary for the public Good.

HE has forbidden his Governors to paſs Laws of immediate and preſſing Importance, unleſs ſuſpended in their Operation till his Aſſent ſhould be obtained; and when ſo ſuſpended, he has utterly neglected to attend to them.

HE has refuſed to paſs other Laws for the Accommodation of large Diſtricts of People, unleſs thoſe People would relinquiſh the Right of Repreſentation in the Legiſlature, a Right ineſtimable to them, and formidable to Tyrants only.

HE has called together Legiſlative Bodies at Places unuſual, uncomfortable, and diſtant from the Depoſitory of their public Records, for the ſole Purpoſe of fatiguing them into Compliance with his Meaſures.

HE has diſſolved Repreſentative Houſes repeatedly, for oppoſing with manly Firmneſs his Invaſions on the Rights of the People.

HE has refuſed for a long Time, after ſuch Diſſolutions, to cauſe others to be elected; whereby the Legiſlative Powers, incapable of Annihilation, have returned to the People at large for their exerciſe; the State remaining in the mean time expoſed to all the Dangers of Invaſion from without, and Convulſions within.

HE has endeavoured to prevent the Population of theſe States; for that Purpoſe obſtructing the Laws for Naturalization of Foreigners; refuſing to paſs others to encourage their Migrations hither, and raiſing the Conditions of new Appropriations of Lands.

HE has obſtructed the Adminiſtration of Juſtice, by refuſing his Aſſent to Laws for eſtabliſhing Judiciary Powers.

HE has made Judges dependent on his Will alone, for the Tenure of their Offices, and the Amount and Payment of their Salaries.

HE has erected a Multitude of new Offices, and ſent hither Swarms of Officers to harraſs our People, and eat out their Subſtance.

HE has kept among us, in Times of Peace, Standing Armies, without the conſent of our Legiſlatures.

HE has affected to render the Military independent of and ſuperior to the Civil Power.

HE has combined with others to ſubject us to a Juriſdiction foreign to our Conſtitution, and unacknowledged by our Laws; giving his Aſſent to their Acts of pretended Legiſlation:

FOR quartering large Bodies of Armed Troops among us:

FOR protecting them, by a mock Trial, from Puniſhment for any Murders which they ſhould commit on the Inhabitants of theſe States:

FOR cutting off our Trade with all Parts of the World:

FOR impoſing Taxes on us without our Conſent:

FOR depriving us, in many Caſes, of the Benefits of Trial by Jury:

FOR tranſporting us beyond Seas to be tried for pretended Offences:

FOR aboliſhing the free Syſtem of Engliſh Laws in a neighbouring Province, eſtabliſhing therein an arbitrary Government, and enlarging its Boundaries, ſo as to render it at once an Example and fit Inſtrument for introducing the ſame abſolute Rule into theſe Colonies:

FOR taking away our Charters, aboliſhing our moſt valuable Laws, and altering fundamentally the Forms of our Governments:

FOR ſuſpending our own Legiſlatures, and declaring themſelves inveſted with Power to legiſlate for us in all Caſes whatſoever.

HE has abdicated Government here, by declaring us out of his Protection and waging War againſt us.

HE has plundered our Seas, ravaged our Coaſts, burnt our Towns, and deſtroyed the Lives of our People.

HE is, at this Time, tranſporting large Armies of foreign Mercenaries to compleat the Works of Death, Deſolation, and Tyranny, already begun with circumſtances of Cruelty and Perfidy, ſcarcely paralleled in the moſt barbarous Ages, and totally unworthy the Head of a civilized Nation.

HE has conſtrained our fellow Citizens taken Captive on the high Seas to bear Arms againſt their Country, to become the Executioners of their Friends and Brethren, or to fall themſelves by their Hands.

HE has excited domeſtic Inſurrections amongſt us, and has endeavoured to bring on the Inhabitants of our Frontiers, the mercileſs Indian Savages, whoſe known Rule of Warfare, is an undiſtinguiſhed Deſtruction, of all Ages, Sexes and Conditions.

IN every ſtage of theſe Oppreſſions we have Petitioned for Redreſs in the moſt humble Terms: Our repeated Petitions have been anſwered only by repeated Injury. A Prince, whoſe Character is thus marked by every act which may define a Tyrant, is unfit to be the Ruler of a free People.

NOR have we been wanting in Attentions to our Britiſh Brethren. We have warned them from Time to Time of Attempts by their Legiſlature to extend an unwarrantable Juriſdiction over us. We have reminded them of the Circumſtances of our Emigration and Settlement here. We have appealed to their native Juſtice and Magnanimity, and we have conjured them by the Ties of our common Kindred to diſavow theſe Uſurpations, which, would inevitably interrupt our Connections and Correſpondence. They too have been deaf to the Voice of Juſtice and of Conſanguinity. We muſt, therefore, acquieſce in the Neceſſity, which denounces our Separation, and hold them, as we hold the reſt of Mankind, Enemies in War, in Peace, Friends.

WE, therefore, the Repreſentatives of the UNITED STATES OF AMERICA, in GENERAL CONGRESS, Aſſembled, appealing to the Supreme Judge of the World for the Rectitude of our Intentions, do, in the Name, and by Authority of the good People of theſe Colonies, ſolemnly Publiſh and Declare, That theſe United Colonies are, and of Right ought to be, FREE AND INDEPENDENT STATES; that they are abſolved from all Allegiance to the Britiſh Crown, and that all political Connection between them and the State of Great-Britain, is and ought to be totally diſſolved; and that as FREE AND INDEPENDENT STATES, they have full Power to levy War, conclude Peace, contract Alliances, eſtabliſh Commerce, and to do all other Acts and Things which INDEPENDENT STATES may of right do. And for the ſupport of this Declaration, with a firm Reliance on the Protection of divine Providence, we mutually pledge to each other our Lives, our Fortunes, and our ſacred Honor.

Signed by ORDER and in BEHALF of the CONGRESS,

JOHN HANCOCK, PRESIDENT.

ATTEST.
CHARLES THOMSON, SECRETARY.

Broadside set in type by John Dunlap, July 4, 1776.

PART ONE

AT PHILADELPHIA in the summer of 1776, the delegates to the Continental Congress courageously signed a document declaring the independence of the Thirteen American Colonies from Great Britain. Not only did the Declaration of Independence create a nation, but it also pronounced timeless democratic principles. Enshrined today in the National Archives Building at Washington, D.C., it memorializes the founding of the United States and symbolizes the eternal freedom and dignity of Man.

By the time the Continental Congress adopted the Declaration in July 1776, the War for Independence had been underway for more than a year. The colonists had finally resorted to armed conflict. Their grievances had come to a head shortly after the French and Indian War (1754-1763) that had depleted the royal treasury and added the financial burden of administering the vast territory acquired from France. Britain levied new, direct taxes in the Colonies and tightened customs controls.

The colonists resented these measures. Some Americans also felt that some sort of conspiracy existed in England to destroy their liberties and self-government. They believed that the mission of the large force of redcoats assigned to the Colonies actually was internal suppression rather than protection from a nonexistent external threat. Particularly aggravating was the realization that the new tax levies supported the redcoat force. Indebtedness to British creditors irritated Southern planters. Commercial interests in the Middle Colonies disliked the prohibition on manufacturing certain products. Frontier settlers and speculators were irked at restrictions on westward expansion and the Indian trade.

Peaceful protest and harassment of tax and customs collectors gave way to rioting and mob violence. In New York and Massachusetts, clashes with British troops culminated in bloodshed. Realizing that some of these disturbances stemmed from agitation in the colonial assemblies, which had enjoyed wide autonomy, the Crown tightened its control over them. Disputes between legislators and the King's officials

became commonplace. In Virginia and Massachusetts, the Royal Governors dissolved the assemblies. In these and a few other provinces the Whigs separated from their Tory, or Loyalist, colleagues, met extralegally and adopted retaliatory measures. Nearly all the Colonies formed special "committees of correspondence" to communicate with each other—the first step toward unified action.

In May 1774, in retaliation for the "Boston Tea Party," Parliament closed the port of Boston and virtually abolished provincial self-government in Massachusetts. These actions stimulated resistance across the land. That summer, the Massachusetts lower house, through the committees of correspondence, secretly invited all 13 Colonies to attend a convention. On September 5, in response, 55 delegates representing 12 colonies, Georgia excepted, convened in Philadelphia at Carpenters' Hall and organized the First Continental Congress.

Sharing common complaints against the Crown, the delegates propounded a wide variety of political opinions. Most agreed that Parliament had no right to control the internal affairs of the Colonies. Moderates believed Parliament should continue to regulate commerce. Others questioned the extent of its authority. A few delegates felt the answer to the problem lay in parliamentary representation. Most suggested legislative autonomy for the Colonies, although none yet openly entertained the idea of complete independence from Great Britain.

After weeks of debate and compromise, Congress adopted two significant measures. The first declared that the American colonists were entitled to the same rights as Englishmen everywhere and denounced any infringement of those rights. The second, the Continental Association, provided for an embargo on all trade with Britain. To enforce the embargo and punish violators, at the behest of Congress, counties, cities, and towns formed councils, or committees, of safety—many of which later became wartime governing or administrative bodies. When Congress adjourned in late October, the delegates resolved to reconvene in May 1775 if the Crown had not responded by then.

The First Continental Congress, Carpenters' Hall, 1774.

In a sense, the Continental Congress acted with restraint, for while it was in session the situation in Massachusetts verged on war. In September, just before Congress met, British troops from Boston had seized ordnance supplies at Charlestown and Cambridge and almost clashed with local militia. The next month, Massachusetts patriots, openly defying royal authority, organized a Revolutionary provincial assembly and a military defense committee. Whigs in three other colonies—Maryland, Virginia, and New Hampshire—had earlier that year formed governments. By year's end, all the Colonies except Georgia and New York had either set up new ones or taken control of those already in existence. During winter 1774-1775, colonial militia units prepared for war.

The crisis came in spring 1775 in Massachusetts. Late on the night of April 18, Royal Governor Gen. Thomas Gage dispatched 600 troops from Boston to seize a major supply depot at Concord. Almost simultaneously, the Boston council of safety, aware of Gage's intentions, directed Paul Revere and William Dawes to ride ahead to warn militia units and citizens along the way of the British approach, as well as John Hancock and Samuel Adams at nearby Lexington. Forewarned, the two men went into hiding.

About 77 militiamen confronted the redcoats when they plodded into Lexington at dawn. After some tense moments, as the sorely outnumbered colonials were dispersing, blood was shed. More flowed at Concord and much more along

Paul Revere's famous ride in April 1775.

the route of the British as they retreated to Boston, harassed most of the way by an aroused citizenry. What had once been merely protest had evolved into open warfare; the War for Independence had begun.

The Second Continental Congress convened in the Pennsylvania State House at Philadelphia May 10, 1775. It created a Continental Army, unanimously elected George Washington as commander in chief, appointed other generals, and tackled problems of military finance and supply. Yet despite these warlike actions, many delegates still hoped for a peaceful reconciliation.

In July, Congress adopted the Olive Branch Petition, a final attempt to achieve an understanding with the Crown. The petition appealed directly to King George III to cease hostilities and restore harmony, but he refused to acknowledge the plea and proclaimed the Colonies to be in a state of rebellion.

During winter 1775-1776, all chance for accommodation vanished. Congress, for the first time representing all Thirteen Colonies because Georgia had sent delegates in the fall, disclaimed allegiance to Parliament, created a navy, and appointed a committee of foreign affairs. The patriots, despite their mounting influence in the provincial assemblies, felt they needed more public support and hesitated to urge a final break with the Crown.

The turning point came in January 1776 with publication in Philadelphia of the pamphlet *Common Sense*, authored anonymously by the recent English immigrant Thomas Paine. He denounced George III for creating the Colonies' miseries, condemned the British constitution as well as the monarchy in general, and exhorted his fellow Americans to declare independence immediately. The pamphlet was purchased by many thousands of people and read by thousands more. It created a furor.

Portrait of George Washington
by James Peale.

The fight on Lexington Common, April 19, 1775, by Howard Pyle.

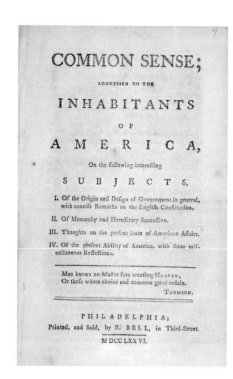

Thomas Paine

From Georgia to New Hampshire, independence became the major topic of discussion and debate. The Revolutionaries won thousands of converts.

In May, Congress boldly authorized the Colonies to form permanent governments. Those that had not done so began to oust Crown officials and draft constitutions. Independence, though not yet officially declared, was for all practical purposes a reality.

The official movement for independence took root in the provincial assemblies. The North Carolina assembly in April 1776 instructed its congressional delegates to vote for the issue should it be proposed. On May 4, Rhode Island announced its independence publicly—the first colony to do so. But Virginia prodded Congress to action. On May 15, a Williamsburg convention declared Virginia independent and authorized its delegation at Philadelphia to propose a similar course for the Colonies. On June 7, the delegation's leader, Richard Henry Lee, introduced the following resolution:

> That these United Colonies are, and of right ought to be, free and independent States, that they are absolved from all allegiance to the British Crown, and that all political connection between them and the State of Great Britain is, and ought to be, totally dissolved.

The resolution incorporated proposals to form foreign alliances and to devise a plan for confederation, which would be submitted to the Colonies for their approval.

Despite the enthusiastic response of many delegates, some objected to the timing. They believed the decision should reflect the desires of the people as expressed through the provincial assemblies and pointed out that the Middle Colonies needed more time for deliberation. On June 10, the moderates obtained a postponement of consideration of the Lee resolution until July 1.

On June 11, the Revolutionaries persuaded Congress to appoint a committee to draft a declaration of independence. Three of its five members, John Adams, Benjamin Franklin, and Thomas Jefferson, were Revolutionaries. Roger Sherman disliked extremism but had recently backed the independence movement. The most unlikely member, Robert R. Livingston, had stood in the front ranks of opposition to Lee's resolution. Possibly he was appointed to exert a moderating effect on its supporters or, conversely, in the hope that the membership would help swing over the conservative New York delegation.

Seven of the Colonies—New Hampshire, Rhode Island, Massachusetts, Connecticut, Virginia, North Carolina, and Georgia—favored independence. New York, New Jersey, Pennsylvania, Delaware, South Carolina, and Maryland were either opposed or undecided. Throughout the month, Revolutionaries in those provinces labored to gain control of the assemblies. Delaware and Pennsylvania, unable to reach a decision, instructed their representatives to vote in their colonies' "best interests." New Jersey issued similar directions but also elected an entirely new and Whig-oriented slate of delegates. The Maryland assembly voted unanimously

The Declaration Committee (l-r): Thomas Jefferson, Roger Sherman, Benjamin Franklin, Robert Livingston, and John Adams, lithograph by Currier & Ives.

for independence and so charged its delegates. The South Carolinians vacillated. The New Yorkers impatiently awaited instructions.

July 1 was the day of decision. The Revolutionaries anticipated an almost unanimous vote for independence. They were disappointed. Following congressional procedure, each colony balloted as a unit, determined by the majority of delegate opinion. Only nine of the Colonies voted affirmatively; Pennsylvania and South Carolina, negatively; New York abstained; and the two delegates present from Delaware deadlocked. Technically the resolution had carried, but the solidarity desirable for such a vital decision was missing. Edward Rutledge of South Carolina moved that the vote be retaken the next day.

That day proved to be one of the most dramatic in the history of the Continental Congress. John Adams of Massachusetts exerted an overwhelming influence. South Carolina, its delegates swayed by Rutledge, reversed its position. Two conservatives among the seven Pennsylvanians, Robert Morris and John Dickinson, cooperated by purposely absenting themselves; the remaining delegates voted three to two in favor. Caesar Rodney, Delaware's third delegate, galloped up to the statehouse after a harrowing 80-mile night ride from Dover through a thunderstorm and broke the Delaware tie. In the final vote, 12 Colonies approved Lee's resolution, New York again abstaining. Congress declared the resolution to be in effect.

For the remainder of July 2 and continuing until July 4, Congress weighed and debated the content of the Declaration of Independence, which the drafting committee had submitted on June 28. Its author was young Thomas Jefferson, who had been in Congress about a year. The committee had chosen him for the task because he was from Virginia, the colony responsible for the independence resolution, and because of his reputation as an excellent writer and man of talent and action.

Jefferson had completed a rough draft in about two weeks. Apparently Franklin and Adams made some minor changes, and Livingston and Sherman expressed no reservations so far as is known. Congress altered the final draft considerably. Most of the changes consisted of refinements in phraseology, and two major passages were deleted. The first, a censure of the people of Great Britain, seemed harsh and needless to most of the delegates. The second, an impassioned condemnation of the slave trade, offended Southern planters as well as New England shippers, many of whom were as culpable as the British in the trade.

The first official document of the American Republic and one of the most influential in human history, the Declaration expressed the spirit of human freedom and affirmed Man's universal rights. Jefferson's goal in drafting it was to compose "an expression of the American mind" in a tone and spirit suitable for the momentous occasion. Stylistically, the Declaration resembled his own preamble to the Virginia constitution and contained an almost identical list of grievances. Its political philosophy was certainly not new. Jefferson had touched on the basic points

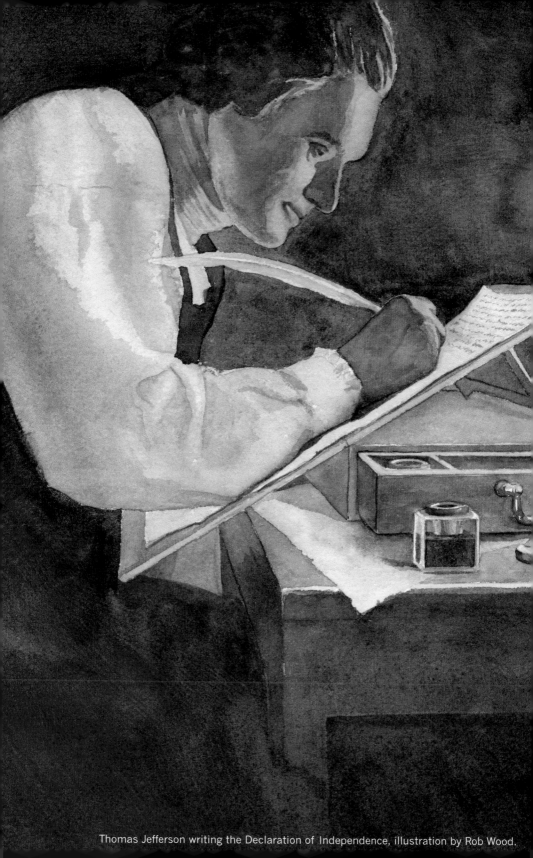

Thomas Jefferson writing the Declaration of Independence, illustration by Rob Wood.

in previous writings, and in essence he echoed George Mason's "Declaration of Rights," published early in June by some Philadelphia newspapers. The Declaration assimilated existing concepts into a concise statement of national doctrine.

Jefferson began the preamble, "When in the course of human events, it becomes necessary for one people to dissolve the political bands which have connected them with another...." He then listed a series of "self-evident" truths—that "all men are created equal" and that they are "endowed by their creator with certain unalienable rights ...." Governments, "deriving their just powers from the consent of the governed," are instituted by men to ensure these rights. When they fail to do so, it is the "right of the people to alter or to abolish" them and to institute new governments. The longest portion of the Declaration is a list of colonial grievances and examples of the King's tyranny. The final section includes a restatement of Lee's resolution and a pledge by the signers of their lives, their fortunes, and their sacred honor to the cause of independence.

On July 4, all the Colonies except New York voted to adopt the Declaration. Congress ordered it printed and distributed to colonial officials, military units, and the press. John Hancock and Charles Thomson, president and secretary of Congress respectively, were the only signers of this broadside copy. On July 8, outside the Pennsylvania State House, the document was first read to the public. During the ensuing celebration, people cheered, bells rang out, and soldiers paraded. At other cities, similar celebrations soon took place. Yet many citizens— the Loyalists, or Tories—could not accept independence now that it had been declared any more than previously when it had been merely a concept. Some would continue to dream of reconciliation. Others would flee from or be driven out of the country. Another sizable group of citizens remained noncommittal.

Four days after obtaining New York's approval of the Declaration on July 15, Congress ordered it engrossed on parchment for signature. At this time, the title was changed from "A Declaration by the Representatives of the United States of America in General Congress Assembled" to "The Unanimous Declaration of the Thirteen United States of America."

The 56 signers did not sign as a group and did not do so on July 4, 1776. The official event occurred on August 2, 1776, when 50 men probably took part. Later that year, five more apparently signed separately, and one added his name in a subsequent year. Not until January 18, 1777, in the wake of Washington's victories at Trenton and Princeton, did Congress, which had sought to protect the signers from British retaliation for as long as possible, authorize printing of the Declaration with all their names listed. At this time, Thomas McKean had not yet penned his name.

The most impressive signature is that of John Hancock, president of Congress, centered over the others. According to tradition, Hancock wrote boldly and defiantly so that King George III would not need spectacles to identify him as a "traitor" and double the reward for his head. The other delegates signed in six

The first public reading of the Declaration of Independence, July 8, 1776.

General George Washington leading the attack at the Battle of Trenton, New Jersey, December 1776, steel engraving, 1876.

John Hancock's Defiance, 1876 lithograph by Currier & Ives.

columns, which ran from right to left. They utilized the standard congressional voting order by colony generally from north to south: New Hampshire, Massachusetts, Rhode Island, Connecticut, New York, New Jersey, Pennsylvania, Delaware, Maryland, Virginia, North Carolina, South Carolina, and Georgia.

Independence had been declared; it still had to be won on the battlefield. The War for Independence was underway, but five more years of struggle and bloody campaigning lay ahead. In 1781, the Colonies achieved military victory, and two years later, Britain in the Treaty of Paris officially recognized the independence proclaimed in 1776. The building of the nation could begin.

Benjamin Franklin, John Adams, and Thomas Jefferson drafting the Declaration, painting by Jean Leon Gerome Ferris.

PART TWO

THE SIGNERS OF THE DECLARATION OF INDEPENDENCE

JOHN ADAMS | MASSACHUSETTS

The subsequent career of Adams—as a diplomat and first vice president and second president of the United States—overshadows those of all the other signers except Jefferson.

Adams was born in 1735 at Braintree (later Quincy), Mass. He graduated from Harvard College in 1755 and for a short time taught school at Worcester, Mass. He considered entering the ministry, but decided instead to follow the law and began its study with a local lawyer. Adams was admitted to the bar at Boston in 1758 and began to practice in his hometown. Six years later, he married Abigail Smith, who was also the first mistress of the White House.

Adams was propelled into the Revolutionary camp by the Stamp Act. In 1765, he wrote a protest for Braintree that scores of other Massachusetts towns adopted. Three years later, he temporarily left his family behind and moved to Boston. He advanced in the law but devoted much of his time to the patriot cause. In 1768, he achieved recognition throughout the Colonies for his defense of John Hancock, whom British customs officials had charged with smuggling.

Adams later yielded to a stern sense of legal duty but incurred some public hostility by representing the British soldiers charged with murder in the Boston Massacre (1770). Ill health forced him to return to Braintree following a term in the colonial legislature (1770-1771), and for the next few years he divided his time between there and Boston.

A three-year stint in the Continental Congress (1774-1777), punctuated by short recuperative leaves and service in the colonial legislature in 1774-1775, brought Adams national fame. Because he was attuned to the temper of Congress and aware that many members resented Massachusetts' extremism, he at first acceded to conciliatory efforts with Britain and restrained himself publicly. When Congress opted for independence, he became its foremost advocate, eschewing conciliation and urging a colonial confederation.

Adams was a member of the five-man committee charged with drafting the Declaration. He defended it from its congressional detractors, advocated it to the wavering, and guided it to passage.

In November 1777, Adams retired from Congress—never to return. He headed back to Braintree intending to resume his law practice. But, before the month expired, Congress appointed him to a diplomatic post in Europe in which he served from 1777 to 1788.

Adams served in France from 1778 to 1785, interrupted only by a visit to the United States in summer 1779, during which he attended the Massachusetts constitutional convention. Independent-minded and forthright, he frequently found himself at odds with fellow diplomats Benjamin Franklin and Arthur Lee and French officials whose policies toward the Colonies he mistrusted. He joined Franklin and John Jay, however, in negotiating the Treaty of Paris (1783), by which Britain recognized the independence of the United States.

Meanwhile, during the preceding three years, Adams had persuaded the Dutch to recognize the Colonies as an independent nation, grant a series of loans, and negotiate a treaty of alliance. As the first American Envoy to Great Britain (1785-1788), he strove to resolve questions arising from the Treaty of Paris and to calm the harsh feelings between the two countries.

Back in the United States, Adams was soon elected as the first vice president (1789-1797), an office he considered insignificant but in which he emerged as a leader of the Federalist Party. During his stormy but statesmanlike presidency (1797-1801), he inherited the deep political discord between the Hamiltonians and Jeffersonians that had taken root during Washington's administration. Adams pursued a neutral course without abandoning his principles. He kept the United States out of a declared war with France and achieved an amicable peace. But he proved unable to unite his party, divided by Hamilton's machinations and the ramifications of the French Revolution.

The Jeffersonians drove the Federalists out of office in 1800, and Adams retired to Quincy. He never lost interest in public affairs and lived to see his son, John

Quincy, become president. John died at age 90 just a few hours after Jefferson, on July 4, 1826—dramatically enough the 50th anniversary of the adoption of the Declaration. His and Abigail's remains are interred in a basement crypt at the United First Parish Church in Quincy.

SAMUEL ADAMS | MASSACHUSETTS

Adams, son of a prosperous and politically active brewer and landowner, was born at Boston in 1722 and attended the Boston Latin School and Harvard College. After graduation in 1740, he first demonstrated his lifelong aversion to normal employment. He studied law for a while and then skipped from job to job, working for a time in his father's brewery, in a counting house, and dissipating a paternal loan in an unsuccessful business venture.

When his father died in 1748 and his mother soon afterwards, Adams inherited a sizable estate, including the family home and brewery. By 1764, when the colonial quarrel with Britain began, he had long since lost the latter. And, during the previous eight years as city tax collector, he had fallen in arrears about £8,000 in his collections. At age 42, unable to support a family, and residing in his rundown birthplace, he was destitute and besieged by creditors. He subsisted mainly on gifts and donations from loyal friends and neighbors.

Then Adams found the only meaningful "occupation" he ever pursued. For almost two decades he had been active in local political clubs, earning a reputation as a writer and emerging as leader of the "popular" party that opposed the conservative aristocracy controlling the Massachusetts government. As clerk in the colonial legislature (1765-1774), he drafted most of the body's official papers and quickly seized the tools of power.

He pounced on the taxation issue raised by the Sugar Act (1764) and Stamp Act (1765), and within a year he and his party fanned popular hatred of the conservatives and gained control of the legislature.

The Townshend Acts (1767), imposing a series of taxes on imports, provided Adams with a new cause for dissent. He urged merchants not to purchase goods from Britain, fomented opposition toward customs officials, inflamed the resentment toward British troops stationed in the colony that led to the Boston Massacre (1770), and humiliated the Royal Governor so much that he was recalled. Adams also authored a circular letter protesting British taxation and advocating united opposition. When, in 1768, the Massachusetts legislature sent it to the 12 other colonial assemblies, the Royal Governor dissolved the legislature, soon a common British practice in America. All these activities, coupled with authorship of scores of newspaper articles and extensive correspondence with prominent persons in the Colonies and England, brought Adams fame.

The conservative reaction of merchants, the legislature, and the populace that surfaced after the repeal of practically all the Townshend Acts in 1770 failed to stifle Adams, though his popularity and influence declined. In perhaps his chief contribution to the Revolution, he kept the controversy alive by filling the columns of the Boston newspapers with reports of British transgressions and warnings of more to come. In 1772, he began constructing the framework of a Revolutionary organization in Massachusetts. He convinced Boston and other towns to create committees of correspondence. The next year, he was appointed to the Massachusetts committee, formed in response to a call from the Virginia House of Burgesses.

Passage of the Tea Act (1773) rekindled the flame of rebellion. Adams helped to incite and probably participated in the "Boston Tea Party," which engendered a series of rebellious incidents throughout the Colonies and pushed them closer to war. Parliament retaliated the next spring by passing a series of acts designed to punish Massachusetts.

Adams urged an intercolonial congress to discuss mutual grievances and plan a united course of action. In June, the Massachusetts House of Representatives resolved to invite the other 12 Colonies to send representatives to Philadelphia in September and also appointed five delegates, including Adams. That same day, the Royal Governor disbanded the legislature for the last time. Before heading for Philadelphia, Adams helped organize the convention that adopted the Suffolk Resolves, which in effect declared Massachusetts to be in a state of rebellion.

Adams served in the Continental Congress until 1781. In the early sessions, most of the time he shrewdly stayed in the background with his fellow Massachusetts delegates, whose radicalism offended most of their colleagues. And, throughout the Congress, he walked in the shadow of John Adams, who dominated the proceedings.

But nothing could match the drama of an episode involving Samuel in the interim between the First and Second Continental Congresses. Back at Lexington, Mass., one night in April 1775, he and Hancock had barely escaped the British force seeking to capture the colonial supply depot at Concord. The outbreak of armed conflict the next dawn marked the beginning of the War for Independence.

In 1779-1780, Adams participated in the Massachusetts constitutional convention. He returned to Boston the next year and entered the state senate (1781-1788), over which he presided. He refused to attend the Constitutional Convention of 1787 because of his objection to a stronger national government and in 1788, unenthusiastically took part in the Massachusetts ratifying convention. A lifetime of public service culminated in his election as lieutenant governor (1789-1793), interim governor in 1793 upon Hancock's death, and governor (1794-1797). Still living in "honest poverty," he died at Boston in 1803 at age 81 and was buried in the Old Granary Burying Ground.

JOSIAH BARTLETT | NEW HAMPSHIRE

Bartlett was born in 1729 at Amesbury, Mass. At age 16, after a common school education and some knowledge of Latin and Greek, he began to study medicine. In 1750, he hung out his shingle at nearby Kingston, N.H., and quickly won a name not only as a general practitioner but also as an experimenter and innovator in diagnosis and treatment.

During the decade or so preceding the outbreak of the War for Independence, Bartlett held the office of justice of the peace, militia colonel, and legislator. In 1774, he joined the Revolutionaries. He became a member of the New Hampshire committee of correspondence and the first provincial congress, which came into being when the Royal Governor disbanded the colonial assembly. Bartlett was elected that same year to the Continental Congress, but tragedy kept him at home. Arsonists, possibly Loyalists, burned his house to the ground. He immediately constructed a new one on the same site.

While in Congress (1775-1776), Bartlett also served on the New Hampshire council of safety. Although he rarely participated in congressional debates, he sat on various committees. He was reelected in 1777 but was too exhausted to attend. He managed in August to lend his medical skills to Gen. John Stark's force of New Hampshire militia and Continental troops. They defeated a predominantly German element of Gen. John Burgoyne's command in the Battle of Bennington, N.Y.—one of the reverses that helped force Burgoyne to surrender two months later at Saratoga, N.Y. Bartlett's last tour in Congress was in 1778-1779, after which he refused reelection because of fatigue.

Bartlett spent the remainder of his life on the state scene. Despite his lack of legal training, he sat first as chief justice of the court of common pleas (1779-1782), then as associate (1782-1788) and chief justice (1788-1790) of the Superior Court. Meantime, in 1788, he had taken part in the state convention that ratified the Federal Constitution, which he strongly favored. The next year, probably on account of his age and the weight of his judicial duties, he declined election to the U.S. Senate. The following year, he became chief executive, or president, of the state. He held that title for two years, in 1793-1794 being named the first governor, as the newly amended constitution redesignated the position.

Bartlett had never lost interest in the field of medicine. In 1790, Dartmouth College conferred on him an honorary degree of Doctor of Medicine. The next year, he founded the New Hampshire Medical Society and became its first president. In 1794, the year before he died in Kingston at age 65, ill health forced his retirement from public life. His remains lie in the Universalist Churchyard in Kingston.

Independence Hall as it appeared in 1776.

Braxton was born in 1736 at Newington Plantation, in King and Queen County, Va. His father was a wealthy and politically influential planter.

In 1755, Braxton graduated from the College of William and Mary and married. His bride died in childbirth in 1757. In 1758, he left for an extended visit to England. He returned to Virginia in 1760 and moved into Elsing Green, an estate in King William County, that his brother George had built for him during his absence. At age 25 in 1761, Carter remarried and entered the House of Burgesses. He served there, except for a term as county sheriff in 1772-1773, until 1775. Meantime, in 1767, he had erected a new home, Chericoke, a couple of miles northwest of Elsing Green.

When the trouble with Great Britain erupted, Braxton sided with the patriots. In 1769, he signed the Virginia Resolves, a document protesting parliamentary regulation of the colony's affairs, and the Virginia Association, a nonimportation agreement. During 1774-1776, he attended various Revolutionary conventions. In 1775, upon dissolution of the royal government, he accepted a position on the council of safety, the temporary governing body.

In spring 1775, Braxton was instrumental in preventing the outbreak of war in Virginia. On April 20, the day after the clashes at Lexington and Concord, Royal Governor Lord John M. Dunmore seized the gunpowder in the Williamsburg magazine. Several colonial militia units prepared to retaliate, but moderate leaders such as George Washington and Peyton Randolph restrained them. Patrick Henry, however, refusing to be pacified, led a group of the Hanover County militia into Williamsburg and demanded the return of the gunpowder or payment for it. Before any hostilities occurred, Braxton, as spokesman for Henry, met with crown official Richard Corbin, and convinced him to pay for the powder.

In fall 1775, Braxton was selected to fill a vacancy in Congress. Arriving at Philadelphia early in 1776, he at first sharply criticized the independence movement, but eventually yielded to the majority and backed the Declaration.

That same year, he urged adoption of a conservative form of state government and expressed such a mistrust of popular government that he lost his congressional appointment. The conservatives, however, elected him to the new state legislature, in which he sat for the rest of his life. For many years, he was also a member of the governor's executive council.

The War for Independence brought financial hardships to Braxton. He had invested heavily in shipping, but the British captured most of his vessels and ravaged some of his plantations and extensive landholdings. Commercial setbacks in later years ruined him. In 1786, though he retained Chericoke, he moved to Richmond where he died in 1797 at age 61. He was buried in the family cemetery adjacent to Chericoke.

CHARLES CARROLL | MARYLAND

O f Irish descent, Carroll was born in 1737 at his father's townhouse, Carroll Mansion, in Annapolis. Jesuits educated him until he reached about age 11. He then voyaged to Europe and studied the liberal arts and civil law at various schools and universities in Paris, elsewhere in France, and in London.

Carroll sailed home in 1765 at age 28 and built a home at Carrollton Manor, a 10,000-acre estate in Frederick County, newly deeded to him by his father. He added "of Carrollton" to his name to distinguish himself from relatives of the same name. For most of his life, however, he preferred for his country residence the family ancestral home, Doughoregan Manor, in Howard County; when in Annapolis, he usually resided at his birthplace. For almost a decade after his return from Europe, barred from public life by his religion, he lived quietly.

In 1773, Carroll became a champion of the patriots through his newspaper attacks on the proprietary governor. The latter was opposing reforms in officers' fees and stipends for Anglican clergy that the lower house of the legislature had proposed. From then on, Carroll took a prominent part in provincial affairs. In 1774-1776, he supported nonimportation measures, attended the first Maryland Revolutionary convention, and served on local and provincial committees of correspondence and the council of safety. In 1776, he and his cousin, John, a priest traveled to Canada with Benjamin Franklin and Samuel Chase on a congressionally appointed committee that sought but failed to obtain a union of Canada with the Colonies.

Carroll and Chase arrived back in Philadelphia June 11 that year, the day after Congress had postponed the vote on Richard Henry Lee's independence resolution (June 7) until July 1. Maryland had refused to commit itself. Carroll and Chase rushed to Annapolis, recruited William Paca's aid, and conducted a whirlwind campaign that persuaded the provincial convention to pass a unanimous independence resolution. It reached Congress just in time to put the colony in the affirmative column on July 1, the day of the first vote. Three days later, Carroll became a delegate and functioned in that capacity until 1778.

Two years before, Carroll had been elected to the state senate, a seat he retained until just after the turn of the century. He was a member of the committee that in 1776 drafted Maryland's constitution. Elected to but not attending the Constitutional Convention of 1787, he allied himself with the Federalists and helped bring about his state's ratification of the Constitution. In 1789-1792, while also in the state senate, he served as a U.S. senator, one of Maryland's first two.

Not reelected to the state senate in 1804, Carroll retired from public life and concentrated on managing his landholdings, consisting of about 80,000 acres in Maryland, Pennsylvania, and New York, and his business interests. The latter included investments in the Patowmack (Potowmack) Company, which established a canal system in the Potomac and Shenandoah Valleys, and its successor, the Chesapeake and Ohio Canal Company. Carroll was also a member of the first board of directors of the Baltimore and Ohio Railroad.

In his final years, the last surviving signer of the Declaration, Carroll spent most of his time at Doughoregan Manor. But he passed the winters in the home of his youngest daughter and her husband in Baltimore. There, in 1832, he died at age 95. His body was interred in the family chapel at Doughoregan Manor.

S on of an Anglican clergyman, Chase was born in 1741 at the farmhouse of his mother's parents on Maryland's Eastern Shore. His mother died at or soon after the birth. Likely Chase's grandparents cared for him until about the time his father took over a parish in Baltimore and provided the youth with his initial education, mainly in the classics.

Between ages 18 and 20, Chase read law with an Annapolis firm and joined the bar in 1761. He entered the colonial/state legislature and retained membership for two decades. From the beginning, he opposed the royal government. Annapolis officials denounced him for his participation in the violent protests of the Sons of Liberty in 1765 against the Stamp Act. In 1774-1775, he took part in the Maryland committee of correspondence, council of safety, and the provincial convention.

In 1774, Chase had joined the Continental Congress. He advocated an embargo on trade with Britain, showed special interest in diplomatic matters, early urged a confederation of the Colonies, defended George Washington from his congressional detractors, and in 1776, journeyed to Montreal with a commission that tried but failed to achieve a union with Canada. When he returned to Philadelphia, Congress had just postponed the vote on the Lee independence resolution. Realizing that Maryland was straddling the fence on the issue, Chase rushed home. Along with Charles Carroll of Carrollton and William Paca, he labored for two weeks to overcome opposition and won a committal to independence from the convention. The Maryland delegates registered it in time for the first congressional vote on July 1. In 1778, Chase lost his office because of adverse publicity generated by the advantage he had taken of knowledge gained in Congress to engage in a profiteering scheme.

In 1783-1784, Chase traveled to London as a state emissary on an unfruitful mission to recover Maryland stock in the Bank of England from two fugitive Loyalists. Upon his return, he resumed his law practice and engaged in various unsuccessful business enterprises that led to bankruptcy in 1789. Meantime, he had reentered politics. In 1785, he had represented Maryland at the Mount Vernon (Va.) Conference, forerunner of the Annapolis Convention. The next year, he moved his family from Annapolis to Baltimore where he soon became chief judge of the Baltimore County criminal court (1788-1795). As a delegate to the Maryland ratifying convention in 1788, he strongly opposed the Constitution, though he later became a staunch Federalist. From 1791 until 1794, while still a county judge, he also held the position of chief justice of the Maryland Superior Court.

Chase achieved his greatest fame as an Associate Justice of the U.S. Supreme Court (1796-1811). He was one of the ablest jurists in the body prior to Chief Justice John Marshall (1801-1835) and delivered many influential opinions. His inability to control his political partisanship while on the bench led to various judicial improprieties and impeachment proceedings against him in 1805. But Congress acquitted him.

Still a Justice, Chase died in Baltimore two months after his 70th birthday. His grave is in St. Paul's Cemetery.

～○◦⌂◦○～

ABRAHAM CLARK | NEW JERSEY

Clark was born in 1726 at his father's farm in what is now Roselle, N.J. In his boyhood, he was too frail for farm work. He received only a minimum of formal education but in his independent study demonstrated a bent for mathematics. When he reached manhood, besides farming his father's land, he took up surveying and informally read law to aid in mediating land disputes. He gained a reputation as the "poor man's counselor" for his willingness to dispense free legal advice or accept produce or merchandise in lieu of a fee.

For many years, he served the Crown as High Sheriff of Essex County and as clerk in the colonial legislature. In 1774-1776, he became a member and secretary of the New Jersey council of safety, attended several Revolutionary conventions, and won election to the provincial assembly. In June 1776, he and four other men replaced the existing congressional delegates who were opposing independence.

Despite poor health and deep concern for his family's welfare and the safety of his home, located not far from an area of British occupation, Clark stayed in Congress throughout the War for Independence and sometimes sat concurrently in the state legislature.

At war's end in 1783, Clark resumed his life in New Jersey. The next year he began a three-year tour in the state legislature, which he represented at the Annapolis Convention (1786). The following year, ill health prevented his attendance at the Constitutional Convention. He subsequently opposed the Constitution until it incorporated the Bill of Rights. In 1787-1789, he returned to the Continental Congress but in 1789-1790, remained in New Jersey as commissioner to settle his state's accounts with the Federal Government. In 1791-1794, he climaxed a long career of alternating state-national service as a representative in the Second and Third Congresses.

Clark was stricken with sunstroke in 1794 and died at age 68 in Rahway. He was buried there in the Presbyterian Cemetery.

GEORGE CLYMER | PENNSYLVANIA

Clymer was orphaned in 1740, a year after his birth in Philadelphia. A wealthy uncle reared and informally educated him and advanced him from clerk to a full-fledged partner in his mercantile firm, which on his death he bequeathed to his ward.

Motivated partly by the impact of British economic restrictions on his business, Clymer adopted the Revolutionary cause and was one of the first to recommend independence. He attended patriotic meetings, served on the Pennsylvania council of safety and in 1773, headed a committee that forced the resignation of Philadelphia tea consignees appointed by Britain under the Tea Act. In 1775-1776, he acted as one of the first two Continental treasurers, even personally underwriting the war by exchanging all his own specie for Continental currency.

In the Continental Congress (1776-1777 and 1780-1782) the quiet and unassuming Clymer made his mark in committee efforts, especially those pertaining to commerce, finance, and military affairs. During and between his two congressional tours, he also served on a series of commissions that conducted important field investigations. In December 1776, when Congress fled from Philadelphia to Baltimore, he remained behind to carry on congressional business. Within a year, after their victory at the Battle of Brandywine, Pa. (Sept. 11, 1777), British troops advancing on Philadelphia detoured for the purpose of vandalizing Clymer's home in Chester County.

After a brief retirement following his last tour in the Continental Congress, Clymer was reelected in 1784-1788 to the Pennsylvania legislature, where he had also served part-time in 1780-1782 while still in Congress. He advocated penal code reform, opposed capital punishment, and represented Pennsylvania in the Constitutional Convention (1787). The next phase of his career consisted of service as a U.S. representative in the First Congress (1789-1791), then appointment as collector of excise taxes on alcoholic beverages in Pennsylvania (1791-1794). In 1795-1796, he sat on a presidential commission that negotiated a treaty with the Indians in Georgia.

During his retirement, Clymer advanced various community projects, including the Philadelphia Agricultural Society, the Philadelphia Academy of Fine Arts, and the Philadelphia Bank. At age 73 in 1813, he died at Summerseat, an estate at Morrisville that he had purchased and moved to in 1806. His grave is in Friends Meeting House Cemetery, Trenton, N.J.

⋙⟡⟐⟡⋘

An anti-Stamp Act demonstration in New Hampshire, 1765.

Ellery was born in 1727 at Newport, his lifelong residence. Like his father, a rich merchant and political leader, he attended Harvard. On his graduation in 1747, he returned home.

During the following two decades or so, he tried several occupations, eventually studying law, which he began practicing in 1770.

By May 1776, when the colonial legislature sent Ellery to the Continental Congress, he had already earned a reputation for his work on local patriotic committees. The next year, Rhode Island initiated popular election of congressional delegates, and Ellery's Newport constituency maintained him in office until 1786, except for 1780 and 1782. In 1780, he remained in Philadelphia as an ex officio member of the board of admiralty, on which he had been sitting. His other committee assignments included those dealing with commercial and naval affairs. In 1785, he turned down the chief justiceship of the Rhode Island Superior Court to remain in Congress, where he had attained commanding seniority.

The next year, Ellery terminated his congressional career to accept an appointment as commissioner of the Continental Loan Office for Rhode Island (1786-1790). In 1790, President Washington appointed Ellery as customs collector for the district of Newport, a position he held for three decades. Although he was a Federalist, he managed to retain office during the Democratic-Republican administrations, probably because of his Revolutionary record and competence.

In his later years, Ellery prospered. He kept active in public affairs and spent many hours in scholarly pursuits and correspondence. Living to 92, he died in 1820 at Newport where his remains are in the Common Ground Cemetery.

Floyd was born in 1734 at present Mastic, Long Island, N.Y. His father, a prosperous farmer of Welsh ancestry, kept the youth busy with chores, and his education consisted only of informal instruction at home. When Floyd was about age 20, his father and mother died, and he inherited a large estate along with the responsibility of caring for his brothers and sisters. Floyd also devoted considerable time to the affairs of the Brookhaven church, served as town trustee (1769-1771), and rose in the Suffolk County militia to a colonelcy in 1775.

The spirited Massachusetts opposition to the Tea Act in the latter half of 1773 and in 1774 created the first major foment in New York. One of the scattered focal points was eastern Long Island, where Floyd lived. He and many of his neighbors attended meetings that extended sympathy and aid to Massachusetts and protested the closing of the port of Boston by the British. Despite such local outbursts, by the end of 1774, New York was one of only two Colonies, Georgia being the other, in which the patriots did not control the government. For this reason, the Revolutionaries operated mainly on a county basis.

In 1774, Suffolk County sent Floyd to the Continental Congress. He remained there until 1777, returned in 1779-1783, and in the interim served in the state senate and on the council of safety. Yielding the floor of Congress to the other New York delegates, he labored without special distinction on a few committees. But worry about the welfare of his family presented a major distraction. In 1776, when British forces occupied Long Island, his family fled and took refuge in Middletown, Conn. The redcoats used his home at Mastic for a barracks, and Loyalists plundered his lands and belongings. When he came back in 1783, he found the fields and timber stripped, the fences destroyed, and the house damaged.

After the war, Floyd sat for several terms in the state senate, attended the constitutional convention of 1801, supported the Federal Constitution, won election in the years 1789-1791 as a representative in the First Congress, served as presidential elector on four occasions, and became a major general in the New York militia.

About this time, Floyd acquired an interest in western lands. He purchased a tract in central New York at the headwaters of the Mohawk River near present Rome; he supplanted this three years later by obtaining a state grant of over 10,000 acres in the area. He spent most of his summers visiting and developing the acreage.

In 1803, in his late sixties, Floyd deeded his Long Island home and farm to his son, Nicoll, and set out with the rest of his family to make a new life on the frontier. During the first year, he built a home at present Westernville, N.Y. There he died at age 86 in 1821 and was buried in the Presbyterian Cemetery.

BENJAMIN FRANKLIN | PENNSYLVANIA

Franklin was born in 1706 at Boston, son of a soap- and candle-maker. He received some formal education but was principally self-taught. After serving an apprenticeship to his father between the ages of 10 and 12, he went to work for his half-brother, James, a printer. In 1721, James founded *The New-England Courant,* the fourth newspaper in the Colonies. Franklin secretly contributed 14 essays to it, his first published writings.

In 1723, Franklin moved to Philadelphia. He spent only a year there and then sailed to London for two more years. Back in Philadelphia, he rose rapidly in the printing industry. He published *The*

Pennsylvania Gazette (1730-1748), but his most successful venture was the annual *Poor Richard's Almanac* (1733-1758). It won popularity in the Colonies, second only to the Bible, and its fame eventually spread to Europe.

By 1748, Franklin had achieved financial independence and gained recognition for his philanthropy and the stimulus he provided to such worthwhile civic causes as libraries, educational institutions, and hospitals. Energetic and tireless, he pursued his deep interest in science and entered politics.

Franklin served as clerk (1736-1751) and member (1751-1764) of the colonial legislature and as deputy postmaster general of the Colonies (1753-1774). He represented Pennsylvania at the Albany Congress (1754) called to unite the Colonies during the French and Indian War. The congress adopted his "Plan of Union," but the colonial assemblies rejected it because it encroached on their powers.

During 1757-1762 and 1764-1775, Franklin resided in England, originally as agent for Pennsylvania and later for Georgia, New Jersey, and Massachusetts. During the latter period, he underwent a political metamorphosis. Until then, primarily concerned with Pennsylvania provincial politics, he distrusted popular movements and saw little purpose in carrying principle to extremes. Until the issue of parliamentary taxation undermined the old alliances, he led the conservative Quaker party in its attack on the Anglican proprietary party and its Presbyterian frontier cohorts. His purpose throughout the years at London had been displacement of the Penn family administration by royal authority—the conversion of the province from a proprietary to a royal colony.

During the Stamp Act crisis, Franklin evolved to celebrated spokesman at London for American rights. Although as agent for Pennsylvania he opposed by every conceivable persuasive means enactment of the bill in 1765, he did not at first realize the depth of colonial hostility. He regarded passage as unavoidable and preferred to submit to it while actually working for its repeal. His nomination of a friend and political ally as stamp distributor in Pennsylvania, coupled with his apparent acceptance of the legislation, armed his proprietary opponents with explosive issues. Their energetic exploitation of them endangered his reputation at home until reliable information was published demonstrating his unabated opposition. Mob resentment threatened his family and new home in Philadelphia until his tradesmen supporters rallied. Subsequently, Franklin's defense of the American position in the House of Commons during the debates over the Stamp Act's repeal restored his prestige at home.

Franklin returned to Philadelphia in May 1775 and immediately became a member of the Continental Congress. Thirteen months later, he served on the committee that drafted the Declaration. According to a traditional anecdote, when he finished signing he declared, "Gentlemen, we must now all hang together, or we shall most assuredly all hang separately." He subsequently contributed to the government in all other important ways and took over the duties of president of the Pennsylvania constitutional convention.

Within less than a year and a half after his return, he set sail once again for Europe, beginning a career as diplomat that would occupy him for most of the rest of his life. In 1776-1779, one of three commissioners, he directed the negotiations that led to treaties of commerce and alliance with France, where the people adulated him. While he was sole commissioner to France (1779-1785), he and John Jay and John Adams negotiated the Treaty of Paris (1783), which ended the War for Independence.

Back in the United States, in 1785-1787, Franklin became president of the Supreme Executive Council of Pennsylvania. At the Constitutional Convention (May 1787), though he did not approve of many aspects of the finished document, he lent his prestige, soothed passions, and compromised disputes. Working on his *Autobiography*, he could look back on a fruitful life as the toast of two continents. Active nearly to the last, in 1787 he was elected as first president of the Pennsylvania Society for Promoting the Abolition of Slavery—a cause to which he had committed as early as the 1730s. His final public act was signing a memorial to Congress recommending dissolution of the slavery system. Shortly thereafter, in 1790 at age 84, Franklin died in Philadelphia and was buried in Christ Church Burial Ground.

ELBRIDGE GERRY | MASSACHUSETTS

Gerry was born in 1744 at Marblehead, Mass. His father was a wealthy and politically active merchant-shipper who had once been a sea captain. Upon graduating from Harvard in 1762, Gerry joined the family business, which consisted of exporting dried codfish to Barbados and Spain. In 1772-1774, he entered the colonial legislature, where he came under the influence of Samuel Adams, and took part in the Marblehead and Massachusetts committees of correspondence. In June 1774, when Parliament closed Boston Harbor and Marblehead became a major port of entry for supplies donated by patriots throughout the Colonies to relieve the Bostonians, he aided in the transshipment.

Between 1774 and 1776, Gerry attended the first and second provincial congresses; served with Samuel Adams and John Hancock on the council of safety that prepared the colony for war; and, as chairman of the committee of supply, raised troops and dealt with military logistics.

Gerry entered the Continental Congress in 1776 and voted for independence in July, but his absence at the formal ceremonies on August 2 necessitated his signing the Declaration later in the year. Until 1779, Gerry sat on and sometimes presided over the congressional treasury board, which regulated Continental finances.

An army procurement agent as well as a merchant-supplier, he utilized information he obtained in Congress to benefit his lucrative business but denounced profiteering and personally adhered to a fair-price schedule. In 1780, as wartime financial problems mounted, however, the delegates resolved to revise the schedule. Gerry's vehement objections led to a quarrel, and he stormed out of Congress and did not reappear for three years. During the interim, he engaged in trade and privateering and saw duty in the lower house of the state legislature.

Back in Congress in 1783-1785, Gerry numbered among those representatives who had possessed talent as Revolutionary agitators and wartime leaders, but who could not effectually cope with the painstaking task of stabilizing the national government. He was experienced and conscientious but created many enemies with his lack of humor, suspicion of the motives of others, and obsessive fear of political and military tyranny. In 1786, his fortune well established, he retired from business and took a seat in the state legislature. The next year, he moved from Marblehead to Cambridge and purchased a confiscated Loyalist estate, where he resided for the rest of his life.

Gerry was one of the most vocal delegates at the Constitutional Convention of 1787. He antagonized practically everyone by his inconsistency and, according to a colleague, "objected to everything he did not propose." At first he advocated a strong central government but ultimately rejected and refused to sign the Constitution, especially because it lacked a bill of rights and because he deemed it a threat to republicanism. He led the drive against ratification in Massachusetts. In 1789, when he changed his mind and announced his intention to support the Constitution, he was elected to the First Congress, where he championed Federalist policies.

Gerry left Congress for the last time in 1793 and retired for four years. During this time, he came to mistrust the aims of the Federalists, particularly their attempts to nurture an alliance with Britain, and sided with the pro-French Democratic-Republicans. In 1797, President John Adams appointed him as the only non-Federalist member of a three-man commission charged with negotiating reconciliation with France, on the brink of war with the United States. During the ensuing XYZ affair (1797-1798), the French foreign minister duped him into believing that his presence in France would prevent war, and he lingered long after the departure of the other disgusted commissioners. Finally, the embarrassed Adams recalled him, amid Federalist vituperation.

In 1800-1803, Gerry met defeat in four bids for the Massachusetts governorship but finally triumphed in 1810-1812. Near the end of his two terms, the Democratic-Republicans passed a devious redistricting measure to ensure their domination of the state senate. In response, the Federalists heaped ridicule on Gerry and coined the term "gerrymander" to describe the salamander-like shape of one of the redistricted areas.

In 1813, Gerry accepted the vice-presidency in James Madison's Democratic-Republican administration. In fall 1814, the 70-year-old politician was stricken fatally while on the way to the Senate. Gerry is buried in Congressional Cemetery at Washington, D.C.

BUTTON GWINNETT | GEORGIA

Gwinnett was likely born in 1735 at the village of Down Hatherly, Gloucestershire, England. He was the son of an Anglican vicar of Welsh ancestry. He probably learned trade and finance from an uncle, a Bristol merchant, and in 1757, moved to Wolverhampton, Staffordshire. In 1759, Gwinnett entered the export shipping business and built up an extensive trade with the American Colonies. The date of Gwinnett's immigration is unknown, but in 1765, he purchased a store in Savannah, Ga. Later that year, he sold it and abruptly switched vocation, borrowing £3,000 to purchase large St. Catherine's Island, located off the Georgia coast near the mainland port of Sunbury. At this time, he probably erected a home on the island. Before long, already deep in debt, he purchased some coastal lands on credit, received grants of others from the colony, and bought slaves to work his holdings. Poachers aggravated his problems by raiding the island's livestock.

Gwinnett's land, slaves, and other possessions were gobbled up by creditors. In 1773, they took over the island but allowed Gwinnett to maintain his home there for the rest of his life. During the war, however, the approach of British vessels that replenished their food supplies from the livestock on the exposed island sometimes forced him and his family to scurry over to Sunbury for temporary refuge.

Meantime, Gwinnett had long since entered politics. In 1768-1769, he had been designated as one of His Majesty's justices of the peace and as a local pilotage commissioner. In 1769-1771, the voters of St. John's Parish elected him to the colonial assembly at Savannah, but he attended only sporadically because of his financial woes. When they worsened, he left public office for five years.

Gwinnett returned on the national level and belatedly joined the patriot side. His friend Lyman Hall, a Sunbury resident and fellow member of the Midway Congregational Church, swung him over, probably beginning in the summer of 1775. The next February, the provincial congress named Gwinnett to the Continental Congress, though he did not arrive in Philadelphia until May. He attended for only about 10 weeks. After he signed the Declaration on August 2, he returned to Georgia, where he hoped but failed to win an army colonelcy in one of the units the state was forming.

In October, Gwinnett was reelected to the Continental Congress but chose not to attend. Instead, during the next five months, he played a key role in drafting the state's first constitution and helped thwart a proposed union of South Carolina and Georgia. Upon the death of the governor, or president of the Executive Council, in March 1777, the council commissioned Gwinnett as acting governor for two months, but he failed to achieve reelection. Before leaving office, he had clashed with controversial Gen. Lachlan McIntosh, an old rival. The result was a pistol duel in May just outside Savannah. Both men suffered wounds, and Gwinnett died a few days later of a gangrenous leg infection. Colonial Park Cemetery in Savannah contains a grave reputed to be his.

A native of Wallingford, Conn., Hall was born in 1724. He graduated from Yale College in 1747 at age 23, returned home, and heeded a family call to the Congregational ministry. In 1749, he began preaching in Bridgeport and adjacent towns. Young and immature, he somehow alienated his congregation. Repentance brought quick reinstatement from dismissal in 1751 and, for a couple of years, he temporarily filled vacant pulpits.

Hall became disillusioned by his ministerial experiences and studied medicine with a local doctor, partially supporting himself by teaching. When his medical training was completed, he moved back to Wallingford and hung out his shingle.

In 1757, the 33-year-old Hall immigrated to Dorchester, S.C., a settlement of New England Puritans not far from Charleston. Within a few months, he joined some of the residents in a relocation that had been underway since 1752, southward to Georgia's coastal Midway District in St. John's Parish (present Liberty County). This area provided more land and a healthier climate.

In 1758, the colonists finished their immigration and founded Sunbury. It evolved into the thriving seaport hub of the surrounding slave-based, rice-indigo economy. Hall maintained a home there, where it was healthier than inland, as well as at Hall's Knoll, the plantation just north of the present town of Midway. Because its plantations skirted malarial swamps, Hall kept busy providing medical treatment, as well as managing his estate.

St. John's Parish became the wealthiest in Georgia where the populace was steeped in the New England tradition of independence. When trouble with Britain erupted in the mid-1760s, the parish, guided by Hall, stood apart in its opposition from virtually all the rest of the colony except for a cluster of Revolutionaries at Savannah led by George Walton and others. Georgia, the last of the Colonies to join the Continental Association, was the youngest, most remote, and most sparsely settled. Also the poorest, it felt less the impact of British economic restrictions. The Loyalist ruling aristocracy of Georgia, regarding the tiny band of Revolutionaries with contempt, resisted their every move.

Hall was appalled by the poor representation of the parishes as a whole and the indecisiveness of Revolutionary conventions he attended at Savannah in summer

1774 and the next January, especially by their failure to send delegates to the Continental Congress. He dejectedly returned to St. John's Parish. It was ready to secede from the colony and proposed an alliance to South Carolina, which refused. In March 1775, the parish held its own convention and sent Hall as its "delegate" to the Continental Congress.

Two months later, Congress admitted Hall as a nonvoting member. In July, Georgia, finally coming into the fold, sanctioned Hall's presence in Congress and appointed four other delegates. Hall served until 1780. Two years earlier, he had moved his family to the north just before British troops ravaged and conquered the Georgia coast. In the process, they destroyed Hall's Knoll and Hall's Sunbury residence and confiscated his property.

When the British evacuated Savannah in 1782, Hall settled there and resumed his medical practice to mend his fortune. The next January, St. John's Parish, where he had maintained ties, elected him to the state legislature. That body in turn awarded him the governorship (1783-1784). His reconstruction-oriented administration, though marred by his purchase of and speculation in lands confiscated from Loyalists, rehabilitated the war-torn state and laid foundations for future growth.

In Hall's final years, he acted for a time as a judge of the inferior court of Chatham County and as a trustee of a proposed state university (at first to be called Franklin College and later the University of Georgia). In 1785, he sold his Hall's Knoll land. Five years later, he moved from Savannah to Burke County and purchased Shell Bluff Plantation on the Savannah River below Augusta. A few months hence, he died and was buried there. His remains are now interred at the Signers' Monument in Augusta.

Boston Massacre, 1770 engraving by Paul Revere.

Independence Hall

Carpenters' Hall

Jefferson wrote the Declaration in this room in the Graff House.

Hancock, born in 1737 at Braintree (present Quincy), Mass., lost his father, a Congregational pastor, at age seven. He spent the next six years with his grandparents at Lexington before joining his guardian, Thomas Hancock, a childless uncle who was one of the richest merchant-shippers in Boston. After studying at Boston Latin School and graduating from Harvard College in 1754, Hancock began working as a clerk in his uncle's business and learned it rapidly. In 1763, he became a partner of his uncle, who died in 1764 and willed him the firm, a fortune that was probably the greatest in New England, and a luxurious house on Beacon Street.

Hancock allied with other merchants in protesting the Stamp Act (1765), and in 1766 inaugurated a long legislative career. But he did not strongly identify with the patriots until 1768 when British customs officials, their courage bolstered by the arrival of a warship in Boston Harbor, charged him with smuggling and seized one of his ships. During the ensuing riots, the terrified customs officials fled to an island in the harbor. A few months later, the first major contingent of British troops sailed into port and created a tense situation that resulted in the Boston Massacre (1770). John Adams ably defended Hancock in court until the British dropped the smuggling charge, but the episode made him a hero throughout the Colonies.

Samuel and John Adams, perceiving the advantages of such a rich and well-known affiliate, welcomed him into their ranks, encouraged his idolatry by the populace, and pushed him upward in the Revolutionary hierarchy. When the first provincial congress met at Salem and Concord in 1774, he acted as its president as well as chairman of the vital council of safety. The second provincial congress convening in 1775 at Cambridge and Concord elected him to the Continental Congress.

From 1775 until 1777, Hancock presided over the Continental Congress. The first year, his egotism created personal embitterment. Blind to his own limitations, particularly his lack of military experience, he unrealistically entertained the hope that he, instead of Washington, would be appointed as commander in chief of the Continental Army.

Only Hancock and Charles Thomson, the president and secretary of Congress, signed the broadside copy of the Declaration, printed the night of its adoption, July 4, 1776, and disseminated to the public the following day. At the formal signing of the parchment copy on August 2, tradition holds that Hancock wrote his name in large letters so that the king would not need spectacles to recognize him as a "traitor." After resigning as presiding officer in 1777, he remained a member of Congress until 1780, though he spent much of his time in Boston and for the rest of his life solidified his political position in Massachusetts. In 1778, as a major general in the militia, he commanded an expedition that failed to recapture Newport, R.I., from the British. He made a more tangible contribution to the war by accepting Continental currency from his debtors, even though his fortune had already been dented by wartime-induced reverses.

In 1780, Hancock gave up his seat in Congress and attended his commonwealth's constitutional convention. He was overwhelmingly elected first governor (1780-1785) and won reelection in 1787-1793. In 1785-1786, he once again sat in Congress. In 1788, he chaired the Massachusetts convention that ratified the U.S. Constitution, which he favored.

Still governor, in 1793 at age 56, Hancock died at Boston. His funeral, one of the most impressive ever held in New England, culminated in burial at Old Granary Burying Ground.

⚬◦◦◦◦

BENJAMIN HARRISON | VIRGINIA

Harrison was born in 1726 at his father's estate, Berkeley, in Charles City County, Va. He matriculated at the College of William and Mary, but left before graduating in 1745 upon his father's death to assume management of the family plantation. In time, his landholdings grew to include eight plantations and other properties, and he also expanded into shipping and shipbuilding. About 1749, he gained admission to the House of Burgesses. He sat there, frequently as speaker, until 1774, when the Royal Governor disbanded the body.

In 1764, the burgesses, learning about the Stamp Act impending in Parliament, named a committee to draw up a protest. As one of the committeemen, Harrison helped pen the document. The next year, however, when the act went into effect, he refused to endorse Patrick Henry's resolutions urging civil disobedience as a countermeasure. Forced to take a stand as the rift with the Crown widened, Harrison cast his lot with the patriots. Between 1773 and 1776, he shared in the tasks of the Revolutionary conventions, the committee of correspondence, and the provincial congresses.

Meantime, in 1774, Harrison had been appointed to the First Continental Congress where he made valuable contributions on the foreign affairs, marine, military, and financial committees. As chairman of the committee of the whole (1776-1777), he chaired the deliberations leading up to the adoption of the Declaration and the early debates on the proposed Articles of Confederation.

In 1777, Harrison withdrew from Congress and entered the lower house of the Virginia legislature where he presided as speaker in 1778-1781. His three terms as governor (1781-1784) reflected the ascendancy in Virginia of the conservatives. Harrison rejoined the legislature (1784-1791), holding the speakership part of the time. In 1788 at the Virginia ratifying convention, he objected to the Federal Constitution because it lacked a bill of rights. Once ratification had occurred, however, he supported the new government. Three years later, Harrison died in his mid-sixties at Berkeley and was buried there in the family cemetery.

The Battle of Trenton, December 1776.

The year after Hart's birth in 1711 at Stonington, Conn., his parents immigrated to New Jersey and settled on a farm in the Hopewell vicinity. Hart was to live there and till the soil all his life. In time, while gaining the sobriquet "Honest John," he acquired considerable property, including grist, saw, and fulling mills and emerged as a civic leader. From the 1750s until the outbreak of the War for Independence in 1775, he worked his way up the political ladder in Hunterdon County and the state. He held the offices of justice of the peace, county judge, colonial legislator (1761-1771), and judge of the New Jersey court of common pleas.

In the legislature's dispute with the Royal Governor, Hart opposed parliamentary taxation and the stationing of British troops in the colony. During 1774-1776, he attended the New Jersey provincial congresses, where he achieved the vice-presidency and won appointment to the council of safety and the committee of correspondence. In June 1776, he and four other delegates replaced the incumbent conservatives in the Continental Congress. The new delegation arrived at Philadelphia just a few days before the votes for independence on July 1 and 2 and cast affirmative ballots.

In August 1776, just after Hart signed the Declaration, he departed to accept the speakership in the lower house of the New Jersey legislature. That winter, during the British invasion of the province, the redcoats wreaked havoc on his farm and mills and drove him into hiding among the hills surrounding the Sourland Mountains. He ended his exile after the American victories at Princeton and Trenton and discovered that his wife had died and his family had scattered. In 1777-1778, he sat again on the council of safety, but failing health forced his retirement. He died the next year at age 69 on his Hopewell farm. He is buried in the First Baptist Church Cemetery at Hopewell.

Born in 1730 at Maybury Hill, an estate on the outskirts of Princeton, N.J., Hewes was the son of a pious and well-to-do Quaker farmer. He received a strict religious upbringing and studied at a local school. After learning trade from a Philadelphia merchant, he entered business for himself. About 1760, anxious to expand his modest fortune, he moved to the thriving seaport town of Edenton, N.C. There, where he was to reside for the rest of his life, he founded a profitable mercantile and shipping firm, and gained prominence.

As a member of the North Carolina assembly (1766-1775), the committee of correspondence (1773), and the provincial assemblies (1774-1775), Hewes helped the Whigs overthrow the royal government. Elected to the Continental Congress in 1774, he vigorously supported nonimportation measures although it meant personal financial loss. By the time of the outbreak of the War for Independence, he had rejected the faith altogether—culminating a trend that had been evolving because of his love of dancing and other social pleasures and his Revolutionary activities.

Hewes originally had opposed separation from Great Britain. Thus it was a disagreeable task for him in May 1776 to present the Halifax Resolves to the Continental Congress. Enacted the month before by the provincial assembly, they instructed the North Carolina delegates to vote for independence should it be proposed. Hewes considered the resolves premature, ignored his state's commitment, and at first opposed Richard Henry Lee's June 7 independence resolution.

As key members of the marine committee, Hewes and John Adams were instrumental in establishing the Continental Navy. When the time came to appoint the nation's first naval captains, the two men clashed. Hewes nominated his friend, John Paul Jones, an experienced seaman who had recently immigrated to Virginia from Scotland. Adams, maintaining that all the captaincies should be filled by New Englanders, stubbornly protested. New England had yielded to the South in the selection of a commander in chief of the Continental Army, and Adams had fostered the selection of the able Virginian George Washington, so he was not about to make a concession on the Navy. Hewes reluctantly submitted. Jones, who was to become the most honored naval hero of the Revolution, received only a lieutenant's commission.

In 1777, Hewes lost his bid for reelection to Congress, one of the few failures in his life, and in 1778-1779, he found solace in the state legislature. In 1779, despite health problems, he accepted reelection to the Continental Congress. A few months after arriving back in Philadelphia and not long before his 50th birthday, overworked and fatigued, he died. His grave is in Christ Church Burial Ground there.

THOMAS HEYWARD, JR. | SOUTH CAROLINA

Son of one of the wealthiest planters in South Carolina, Heyward was born in 1746 at Old House Plantation in St. Helena's Parish (later St. Luke's Parish and present Jasper County) near the Georgia border about 25 miles northeast of Savannah. In 1771, following five years of study in London, he began practicing law. The next year, his parish sent him to the colonial legislature (1772-1775), which was feuding with the Royal Governor over parliamentary taxation. In 1773, he settled down at White Hall Plantation near his father's residence.

While a legislator, Heyward apparently joined the Revolutionaries, for in the summer of 1774, he attended a provincial convention that chose delegates to the Continental Congress. During 1775-1776, he was active in the first and second provincial congresses and on the council of safety and the committee that drafted a state constitution.

In the Continental Congress (1776-1778), he signed the Articles of Confederation and the Declaration. At the end of his tour, he journeyed to Charleston and resided in the townhouse he had inherited from his father. He became a circuit court judge; represented Charleston in the state legislature; and held a militia captaincy.

In 1779, Heyward was wounded during Brig. Gen. William Moultrie's repulse of a British attack on Port Royal Island, along the South Carolina coast near Heyward's home. In 1780, the British plundered White Hall and carried off all the slaves. When they took Charleston, they captured Heyward, who was helping defend the city. He was imprisoned at St. Augustine, Fla., until July 1781. Shortly before his release, he celebrated Independence Day by setting patriotic verses to the British national anthem. "God Save the King" became "God save the thirteen States," a rendition that soon echoed from New Hampshire to Georgia.

From 1782 until 1789, Heyward resumed his position of circuit court judge, concurrently serving two terms in the state legislature (1782-1784). In 1785, he helped found and became the first president of the Agricultural Society of South Carolina. He devoted most of his remaining days, except for attendance in 1790 at the state constitutional convention, to managing his plantation; he sold his Charleston townhouse in 1794. He died in 1809 at age 62 and was interred in the family cemetery at Old House Plantation.

WILLIAM HOOPER | NORTH CAROLINA

Hooper was born in Boston, Mass., in 1742, the son of William Hooper, a Scottish immigrant and Congregationalist clergyman who five years later transferred to the Anglican Church. Groomed for the ministry, Hooper undertook seven years of preparatory education at Boston Latin School. This qualified him in 1757 to enter Harvard College in the sophomore class. He graduated three years later but, to the chagrin of his father, rejected the ministry as a profession. He further alienated his Loyalist father and isolated himself from his family by taking up the study of law under James Otis, a brilliant but radical lawyer.

In about 1764, Hooper sought his fortune at Wilmington, N.C. He resided either in Wilmington or at his nearby estate, Finian, on Masonboro Sound, rode the circuit from court to court, and built up a clientele among the wealthy planters of the lower Cape Fear region. He harbored political aspirations and by 1770-1771 had become deputy attorney general of North Carolina.

Protecting his own economic interests and political goals, Hooper sided with Royal Governor William Tryon in a conflict between the government and a group of North Carolina frontiersmen known as the Regulators. They were rebelling against governmental corruption and oppression and high legal and other fees. Hooper urged the of force, and in 1771, he accompanied the government forces that defeated the rebels in the Battle of Alamance.

Within a few years, Hooper's allegiance to the royal government waned. At the time of his election to the colonial assembly (1773-1775), the act providing for the colony's court system was about to expire. The assembly attempted to attach to the new court act a clause by which the colony could confiscate American property owned by foreign debtors, including inhabitants of Great Britain. The Royal Governor blocked the bill, and a four-year struggle for control of the colony ensued. Hooper, though deprived of his income as a lawyer and dependent upon his wife's small fortune, championed the cause of the assembly.

Hooper rose to a leadership position among the Whigs though he disapproved of extremism. In a letter dated April 1774 to his friend James Iredell, he prophesized the Colonies' break with Great Britain, the earliest known prediction of independence. This won for Hooper the epithet, "Prophet of Independence." In the summer after the Royal Governor had dissolved the colonial assembly, he helped organize and presided over an extralegal conference at Wilmington. It voted to convene a provincial assembly, which met in August at New Bern and elected delegates, one of whom was Hooper, to the Continental Congress. Later that same year, he became a member of the committee of correspondence.

During 1774-1777, Hooper divided his time between Congress, where he gained a reputation as an orator, and the North Carolina provincial assembly, in which he labored to set up a state government. In 1777, the financial difficulties with his law practice and a desire to be near his family prompted him to resign from Congress and return to Wilmington. He was immediately elected to the state legislature and served there almost continuously until 1786.

In 1780, the British invaded North Carolina. Hooper moved his family from Finian into Wilmington for safety, but in January 1781, while he was away on business, the city fell to the enemy. Upon the British evacuation of the Wilmington area, in November, Hooper returned to find most of his property, including Finian, in ruins. He rejoined his family who had fled to Hillsborough, which was his home for the rest of his life.

During the aftermath of the Revolution, Hooper lost favor with the public. Unable to adjust to the rise of republicanism in the state, he adopted a conservative stance. His aristocratic pretensions, forgiving attitude toward Loyalists, and lack of faith in the common people undermined his popularity. In 1788, he strenuously campaigned for state ratification of the Federal Constitution, which occurred early in 1789. By this time, he was in ill health and despondent but lingered on for nearly two years. He died in 1790 in his late forties. His remains rest today at Guilford Courthouse National Military Park in Greensboro.

⟶⟵◦◦⟶⟵

STEPHEN HOPKINS | RHODE ISLAND

Born in 1707 at Providence and equipped with but a modicum of basic education, Hopkins grew up in the adjacent agricultural community of Scituate and earned his living as a farmer and surveyor. In 1731, when Scituate Township separated from Providence, he plunged into politics. During the next decade, he held the following elective or appointive offices: moderator of the first town meeting, town clerk, president of the town council, justice of the peace, justice and clerk of the Providence County court of common pleas, legislator, and speaker of the house.

In 1742, about two years after he and his brother, Esek, founded a mercantile shipping firm, Hopkins moved back to Providence.

For the next three decades, he built up his business and would probably have acquired a fortune had he not supported a variety of civic enterprises and broadened his political activities. He continued in the legislature, served as assistant and chief justice of the Superior Court and ten-time governor, and represented Rhode Island at various intercolonial meetings. At the Albany Congress (1754), he cultivated a friendship with Benjamin Franklin and assisted him in framing a plan of colonial union that the congress passed but the Colonies rejected.

Hopkins took over leadership of the colony's radical faction, supported by Providence merchants. For more than a decade, it bitterly fought for political supremacy in Rhode Island with a conservative group in Newport, led by Samuel Ward, a political enemy of Hopkins.

Hopkins was a man of broad interests, including humanitarianism, education, and science, and he exerted his talents in many fields. About 1754, he helped set up a public subscription library in Providence. He acted as first chancellor of Rhode Island College (later Brown University), founded in 1764 at Warren, and six years later was instrumental in relocating it to Providence. He also held membership in the Philosophical Society of Newport. Strongly opposing slavery, in 1774 he authored a bill enacted by the Rhode Island legislature that prohibited the importation of slaves into the colony—one of the earliest antislavery laws in the United States.

Hopkins had long sided with the Revolutionaries. In 1762, he helped found the influential *Providence Gazette and Country Journal* and two years later contributed an article entitled, "The Rights of the Colonies Examined," which criticized parliamentary taxation and recommended colonial home rule. Issued as a pamphlet the next year, it circulated throughout the Colonies and Great Britain and established Hopkins as one of the earliest of the patriot leaders. He sat on the Rhode Island committee of correspondence and carried his duties on in the legislature and Superior Court while a member of the Continental Congress (1774-1776). He served on the committees that prepared the Articles of Confederation and that created the Continental Navy and appointed Esek Hopkins as its commander in chief. Ill health compelled Stephen to retire in September 1776, a month after he signed the Declaration.

Hopkins declined subsequent reelections to Congress but sat in the state legislature for a time and took part in several New England political conventions. He withdrew from public service about 1780 and died five years later in Providence at age 78. He was interred in the North Burial Ground.

Hopkinson was born at Philadelphia in 1737. His father, who died when he was 14, was a prominent lawyer-jurist, politician, and civic leader. Upon graduation from the College of Philadelphia (later part of the University of Pennsylvania) in 1757, young Hopkinson studied law under Benjamin Chew, attorney general of the province, and four years later joined the bar. In 1763, he obtained the position of customs collector at Salem, N.J. Three years hence, after failing in business, he sailed to England to seek an appointment as colonial customs collector through the influence of friends and relatives, though he was unsuccessful in his vocational quest.

Back in Philadelphia, Hopkinson operated a store and married in 1768. Four years later, he became the customs collector at New Castle, Del. About 1774, he took up residence at the home of his father-in-law in Bordentown, N.J., practiced law, and began a two-year tour in the legislature. His later offices included: chairman of Philadelphia's Continental Navy Board (1777-1778), treasurer of loans (1778-1781), judge of the admiralty court of Pennsylvania (1779), and federal circuit judge for the eastern district of the state (1789-1791).

During his busy public career, the ambitious Hopkinson managed to leave his stamp on the fields of music, art, and literature. Between 1757 and 1773, Hopkinson contributed numerous poems and essays to various periodicals. The following year, he began advancing the patriot cause. A profusion of widely read and influential pamphlets, essays, and letters, often presented allegorically, derided and ridiculed the British and the Loyalists, outlined colonial grievances, and encouraged the colonists. *The Prophecy,* written in 1776 before the adoption of the Declaration of Independence, predicted that event. After the war, Hopkinson continued to treat political and social themes and became one of the best known American writers.

While a federal circuit judge, Hopkinson died in Philadelphia at age 53. He was buried in Christ Church Burial Ground.

Born in 1731 at Windham (present Scotland), Conn., Huntington grew up on a farm, received a limited education, and at age 16 began work as a cooper. But his ambition soon pushed him onward. He independently studied borrowed legal tomes, won admittance to the bar about 1758, and set up practice. Two years later, he moved to nearby Norwich. As time went on, he prospered in the law and became a community leader.

In 1764, Huntington began his public career in the Connecticut legislature. The next year, he was appointed as King's Attorney of the colony and won election as justice of the peace for New London County. He occupied these positions for practically the entire decade or so prior to the outbreak of the War for Independence in 1775. Meantime, two years earlier, the colonial legislature had named him as a judge of the Connecticut Superior Court, an appointment renewed annually for a decade.

In 1774, Huntington resigned as King's Attorney and joined the front ranks of the Revolutionaries. The next year, he became a member of the upper house of the legislature (1775-1784) and entered national politics when he became a delegate to the Continental Congress. In fall 1776, fatigue and health worries caused him to return to Connecticut. Between then and 1783, plagued with spells of illness, he attended congressional sessions intermittently (1778, 1779-1781, 1783), often returning home to recuperate. Despite this burden, he assumed the heavy responsibilities of President of Congress (1779-1781), presiding on March 1, 1781, when the Articles of Confederation were adopted.

Huntington's "retirement" when he returned to Connecticut in 1783 after eight years of service to the nation, turned out to involve 12 years of vigorous activity. Even while he had been in Congress, he had served his state in various other ways, and all his legislative and other positions had been held open for him. A succession of appointive and elective offices followed: chief justice of the Superior Court (1784), lieutenant governor (1785), and governor (1786-1796). In the latter capacity, he led the battle for Connecticut's ratification of the Federal

Constitution and improved the educational system. As one of Connecticut's seven first presidential electors, in 1789 he won two "favorite son" votes for the presidency.

In the 1780s, Huntington received honorary degrees from Princeton, Yale, and Dartmouth and was appointed one of the original trustees of Plainfield (Conn.) Academy. Before that, he had acted as adviser to the president of Yale.

In 1796 at age 65, still governor, he died at his home in Norwich and was interred in the Old Burial Ground.

⋙∘≪

THOMAS JEFFERSON | VIRGINIA

As author of the Declaration of Independence, influential political theorist, cofounder of the Democratic-Republican Party, Virginia legislator and governor, first U.S. secretary of state, second vice president, and third president, Jefferson has left an indelible impression on our political system and philosophy. Beyond that, he laid the basis for the westward expansion of the nation, and two of his disciples, Madison and Monroe, followed him into the White House.

Like most successful politicians, Jefferson created his share of enemies and felt the sting of failure. He lacked the aggressiveness and charisma of many leaders. To compensate for his basic shyness and his deficiencies as a speaker, he mastered written expression and learned to exercise administrative power. His governorship ended ignominiously. And his vision of an agricultural America, peopled by well-educated and politically astute yeoman farmers, was never to be realized. Yet none of these factors diminishes his stature or undermines his achievements.

Jefferson was born in 1743 at Shadwell, a frontier plantation in Goochland (present Albemarle) County, Va. Two years later his father, Peter, a self-made surveyor-magistrate-planter, moved his family to Tuckahoe Plantation near Richmond. Young Jefferson passed most of his boyhood there, beginning his elementary education with private tutors. In 1752, when he was about nine years old, the family returned to Shadwell. His father died five years later and had bequeathed him almost 3,000 acres.

In 1760, at age 17, Jefferson matriculated at the College of William and Mary in Williamsburg. He graduated in 1762, studied law locally under George Wythe, and in 1767, was admitted to the bar.

At Shadwell, Jefferson assumed the civic responsibilities and prominence his father had enjoyed. In 1770, when fire consumed the structure, he moved to his nearby estate, Monticello, where he had already begun building a home.

Meanwhile, in 1769 at age 26, Jefferson had been elected to the House of Burgesses in Williamsburg. He was a member continuously until 1775 and aligned himself with the anti-British group. Jefferson concentrated his efforts in committee work rather than in debate. He drafted many of the Revolutionary documents adopted by the House of Burgesses.

Jefferson utilized the same working methods in the Continental Congress (1775-1776), where his decisiveness in committee contrasted markedly with his silence on the floor. His colleagues, however, rejected several of the documents he drafted his first year because of their extreme anti-British tone. But, by the time he returned the following May, the temper of Congress had changed drastically. In June, though only 33 years old, he was assigned to the five-man committee chosen to draft the Declaration of Independence. In September, Jefferson returned to Virginia, anxious to be nearer home and feeling he could make a deeper political mark there.

A notable career in the House of Delegates (1776-1779), the lower house of the legislature, followed. There Jefferson took over leadership of the "progressive" party; highlights of this service included revision of the state laws (1776-1779), in which Jefferson collaborated with George Wythe and Edmund Pendleton, and authorship of a bill for the establishment of religious freedom in Virginia, introduced in 1779 but not passed until 1786.

Although hampered as governor (1779-1781) by wartime conditions and constitutional limitations, Jefferson proved to be a weak executive. When the British invaded the state in the spring of 1781, the situation became chaotic. On June 3, while the legislature was meeting in Charlottesville because the redcoats held Richmond, Jefferson recommended the combining of civil and military agencies under Gen. Thomas Nelson, Jr., and virtually abdicated office. Although later formally vindicated for his abandonment of the governorship, the action fostered a conservative takeover of the government, and his reputation remained clouded for some time.

Jefferson stayed out of the limelight for two years. In 1783, he reentered Congress, which the next year sent him to Paris to aid Benjamin Franklin and John Adams in their attempts to negotiate commercial treaties with European nations. During his five-year stay, Jefferson succeeded Franklin as minister to France (1785-1789), gained various commercial concessions from and strengthened relations with the French, visited England and Italy, absorbed European culture, and observed the beginnings of the French Revolution.

In the years that followed, Jefferson filled the highest offices in the land: secretary of state (1790-1793), vice president (1797-1801), and two-term president (1801-1809). He occupied these positions as much out of a sense of civic and party duty as personal ambition. Aggravating normal burdens and pressures were his bitter feuds with Alexander Hamilton on most aspects of national policy, and the vindictiveness of Federalist attacks. Jefferson took considerable satisfaction, however, from his many accomplishments. Among these was the cofounding with James Madison of the Democratic-Republican Party, which in time drove the Federalists out of power.

In 1809, Jefferson retired for the final time to Monticello. He retained his health and varied interests and corresponded with and entertained statesmen, politicians, scientists, explorers, scholars, and Indian chiefs. His pet project during most of his last decade was founding the University of Virginia (1819) in Charlottesville.

Painfully distressing to Jefferson was the woeful state of his finances. His small salary in public office, the attendant neglect of his fortune and estate, general economic conditions, and debts he inherited from his wife had taken a heavy toll. He lived more frugally than was his custom in an attempt to stave off disaster and sold off as many of his lands and slaves as he could. But when a friend defaulted on a note for a large sum, Jefferson fell hopelessly into debt and was forced to sell his library to the government. It became the nucleus of the Library of Congress.

Jefferson died at age 83, only a few hours before John Adams on July 4, 1826, the fiftieth anniversary of the adoption of the Declaration of Independence. For his tombstone at Monticello, he chose three accomplishments that he wanted to be remembered for: authorship of the Declaration of Independence, the Virginia Statute for Religious Freedom, and the founding of the University of Virginia.

Minute men marching to the fight.

Lee, a member of one of the most famous families in Virginia and U.S. history and the son of planter Thomas Lee, was born in 1734 at the family estate, Stratford Hall in Westmoreland County, Va. He was educated by a private tutor and never attended college. In 1750, upon his father's death, he inherited Coton, an estate in Fairfax County. Seven years later, newly created Loudoun County absorbed Coton. At that time, the colonial legislature nominated him as Loudoun lieutenant. The next year he moved to Coton and became trustee of the newly incorporated village of Leesburg, named after him or his brother Philip Ludwell, both local landowners. For the next decade, Francis Lightfoot represented the county in the House of Burgesses.

In 1769, Lee married Rebecca Tayloe and moved to Menokin, a new home his wife's father had built, and sat again with the burgesses until 1774.

Lee had joined the Revolutionary movement early on. From the time of the Stamp Act (1765) until the outbreak of war a decade later, he participated in most of the Virginia protests and assemblies. He rarely debated on the floor in Congress (1775-1779), but often opposed the position of his brother, Richard Henry, and served on the military and marine committees as well as that charged with drafting the Articles of Confederation.

In 1779, weary of office and longing for the peace and quiet of Menokin, Lee left Congress. Except for a few years in the state legislature, he abandoned public service altogether and lived quietly. In 1797 at age 62, he died. Burial took place in the Tayloe family graveyard at Mount Airy.

Lee was born in 1732 along the Potomac shore at Stratford Hall. His initial tutorial education was supplemented by extensive study at Wakefield Academy in Yorkshire, England, and a tour of northern Europe. He sailed home about 1751 at age 19, the year after his father's death, and resided with his eldest brother, Philip Ludwell, at Stratford Hall. In 1757, Richard Henry began building and soon occupied Chantilly on land leased from his brother.

Following family tradition, Lee had committed himself to politics. In 1757 at age 25, he had become justice of the peace for Westmoreland County. The following year, he moved up to the House of Burgesses and sat there until 1775. One of the first to oppose Britain, he early allied with Patrick Henry. As a protest against the Stamp Act (1765), Lee drew up the Westmoreland Association (1766), a nonimportation agreement signed by some of the citizens of his county. The next year, he denounced the Townshend Acts. And a year later, he proposed in a letter to John Dickinson of Pennsylvania that the individual colonies set up committees to correspond with each other—an idea that did not come to fruition for five years.

In 1769, when Lee and Henry penned an address to the king protesting several actions of Parliament, the Royal Governor disbanded the House of Burgesses. Lee thereupon met with other patriots and helped frame the Virginia Association, a nonimportation agreement. Many other colonies formed similar associations, but in 1770, Parliament repealed most of the duties, and the protest spirit subsided.

In March 1773, when anti-British feeling flared once again, Lee, Henry, and Jefferson organized a Virginia committee of correspondence and invited the other colonies to do likewise. Learning of the British closing of Boston Harbor in May 1774, they persuaded their colleagues to declare as a protest, a day of fasting and prayer. The Royal Governor again dissolved the burgesses. The Revolutionaries drew up a new nonimportation agreement and resolved to appeal to the other colonies for an intercolonial congress. But, before such action could be taken, Virginia received an invitation from Massachusetts to send representatives to a congress to be held in September in Philadelphia—the First Continental Congress. Virginia's first provincial assembly met in August and designated seven delegates, including Lee and Henry.

Lee's outstanding congressional act was the introduction on June 7, 1776 of the resolution for independence from Britain, seconded by John Adams. This document, Lee's condensed redraft of one forwarded him by a convention that had met in Williamsburg on May 15, proposed severing relations with Britain, the forming of foreign alliances, and preparation of a plan for confederation. On June 13, Lee journeyed back to Virginia and did not return and sign the Declaration until sometime after the formal ceremony on August 2. Like his brother Francis Lightfoot, in 1777 he also subscribed to the Articles of Confederation. After 1776, his influence in Congress waned, and three years later, ill health forced his resignation.

As a state legislator (1780-1784), Lee joined the conservative faction, which represented the interests of the large planters. A member of Congress again in 1784-1789, he served in 1784-1785 as its president. In 1787, though elected to the Constitutional Convention, he refused to attend and led congressional opposition to the Constitution, especially because of the absence of a bill of rights. Although he was well aware of the deficiencies of the Articles of Confederation, he and others feared a stronger central government. Lee's *Letters of the Federal Farmer to the Republican,* the collective title for two pamphlets outlining his objections to the Constitution, epitomized antifederalist sentiment.

In 1789, Lee entered the U.S. Senate, but because of failing health resigned in 1792, the year after the Bill of Rights was incorporated into the Constitution. He died at Chantilly in 1794 at age 62. His grave is in the Lee family cemetery near Hague, Va.

⋯◦⟨⟩◦⋯

FRANCIS LEWIS | NEW YORK

Lewis was born in 1713 at Llandaff, Glamorganshire, Wales. Orphaned at an early age and raised by relatives, he studied at Westminster School in London and then took employment with a local firm. In 1738, deciding to go into business for himself, he set up branches in New York and Philadelphia and for a few years shuttled between those cities and northern European ports.

During the French and Indian War, in 1756, while functioning as a clothing contractor for British troops at Fort Oswego, in present New York, Lewis was taken captive and sent to France for imprisonment. Upon his release, apparently in 1763, as recompense, the British government awarded him a large land grant in America. He returned to New York City, reentered business, and quickly earned a fortune. In 1765, he retired to the village of Whitestone (now part of Flushing) on Long Island, but in 1771, he temporarily returned to New York City to help his son enter the business world.

Back home, Lewis devoted most of his energies to the Revolutionary movement, which he had joined in 1765 by attending the Stamp Act Congress. In 1774, he became a member of the New York Revolutionary Committee of Fifty-one and later the Committee of Sixty, attended the provincial convention, and subsequently helped set up the state government.

In the Continental Congress (1775-1779), Lewis served on the marine, foreign affairs, and commerce committees, as well as sitting on the Board of Admiralty and engaging in troop supply matters. Because of Tory dominance in New York, Lewis and the other delegates were instructed not to vote for independence on July 1 and 2, 1776, but Lewis signed the Declaration on August 2.

When the British invaded Long Island in 1776, they destroyed Lewis's home in Whitestone and took his wife into custody. She was eventually released in an exchange for wives of British officials, but the hardships she had endured ruined her health and brought about her death in 1779. Grief-stricken, Lewis immediately left Congress, but remained on the Board of Admiralty until 1781, at which time he abandoned politics altogether. He died in 1802 at age 89 in New York City where he was buried in an unmarked grave in the yard of Trinity Church.

Livingston was born in 1716 at his father Philip's townhouse in Albany and spent most of his childhood there or at the family manor at Linlithgo, about 30 miles to the south.

Upon receiving a degree from Yale in 1737, Livingston entered the import business in New York City. Three years later, he married and moved to Manhattan. He built up a fortune, particularly as a trader-privateer during the French and Indian War (1754-1763). In 1764, though retaining his Manhattan home, he acquired a 40-acre estate on Brooklyn Heights overlooking the East River and New York Harbor.

While prospering as a merchant, Livingston devoted many of his energies to humanitarian and philanthropic endeavors. Among the organizations he fostered, financially aided, or helped administer were King's College (later Columbia University), the New York Society Library, St. Andrew's Society, the New York Chamber of Commerce, and New York Hospital.

Livingston was also a proponent of political and religious freedom. As a New York City alderman (1754-1763), he identified with the popular party that opposed the aristocratic ruling class of the colony. In a decade of service (1759-1769) in the colonial legislature, he stood behind the Whigs in their quarrel with the Royal Governor and attended the Stamp Act Congress in 1765.

In the 1769 elections, the Tories gained control of the legislature. In his bid for reelection, Livingston, fearful of the rise of extremism among the populace, attempted to unite the moderate factions. Defeated in New York City, which from then on was Tory-dominated, he managed to obtain reelection from the Livingston Manor district. The new assembly, claiming he could not represent an area in which he did not reside, unseated him.

In 1774, Livingston became a member of the Committee of Fifty-one, an extralegal group that selected New York City delegates to the Continental

Congress, one of whom was Livingston. He also served on the Committee of Sixty, formed to enforce congressional enactments. The next year, he won election to the Committee of One Hundred, which governed New York City temporarily until the first provincial congress of the colony met later that year.

Between 1774 and 1778, Livingston divided his time between the Continental Congress and the New York provincial assembly/legislature. In Congress he sat on committees dealing with marine commerce, finance, military, and Indian matters. He was absent on July 1-2, 1776, even though the New York delegates abstained from voting on the independence issue, but on August 2, he signed the Declaration.

After their defeat in the battle of Long Island (August 27, 1776), Washington and his officers met at Livingston's residence in Brooklyn Heights and decided to evacuate the island. Subsequent to the ill-fated peace negotiations at Staten Island in September, the British occupied New York City and utilized Livingston's Manhattan home as a barracks, his Brooklyn Heights residence as a Royal Navy hospital, and confiscated his business interests. He later sold some of his remaining property to sustain public credit. Livingston and his family had fled to Esopus (later Kingston), N.Y., where the state capital was temporarily located, before moving to nearby Poughkeepsie.

Livingston died at age 62 in 1778. At the time, though in poor health, he was still in Congress, then meeting at York, Pa. He is buried in Prospect Hill Cemetery in York.

The silver inkstand believed to be used by the signers.

The son of Thomas Lynch, Sr., a rich rice planter, Lynch was born in 1749 at Hopsewee Plantation, on the North Santee River in Prince George's Parish (present Georgetown County), S.C. After attending the Indigo Society School at Georgetown from 1764 until 1772, he studied abroad at Eton and Cambridge and read law in London. Upon his return home, deciding not to engage in the law, he married and settled at Peach Tree Plantation. A gift from his father, it was situated in St. James Parish (present Charleston County) on the South Santee River near Hopsewee.

As heir of one of the most fervent Revolutionaries and influential men in the colony, Lynch naturally took a deep interest in politics and enjoyed strong support from the electorate. During 1774-1776, while his father served in the Continental Congress, he labored on the home front, attending the first and second provincial congresses, the first state legislature, and sitting on the state constitutional committee.

In 1775, he accepted a captaincy in the First South Carolina Regiment of Continentals. On a recruiting trip to North Carolina, Lynch contracted bilious fever. This ended his military days and rendered him a partial invalid for his few remaining years.

Early in 1776 at Philadelphia, the elder Lynch suffered a stroke that virtually incapacitated him for further public service. In the spring, his concerned colleagues in South Carolina elected his son to the Continental Congress, probably so that he could care for his father and act officially on his behalf. Although ill himself, Lynch made the trip to Philadelphia. He stayed there throughout the summer, long enough to vote for and sign the Declaration of Independence at age 27. His father was unable to take part in the ceremony. The two were the only father-son team that served concurrently in the Continental Congress.

By the end of the year, the failing health of both men compelled them to start homeward. En route, at Annapolis, Md., a second stroke took the life of the senior Lynch. His son, broken in spirit and physically unable to continue in politics,

The Assembly Room in Independence Hall.

retired to Peach Tree. Late in 1779, he and his wife, heading for southern France in an attempt to regain his health, boarded a ship bound for the West Indies that foundered, and the couple died.

———⊸∘⟨⟨⟩∘⊸———

THOMAS MCKEAN | DELAWARE

Of Scottish-Irish ancestry, McKean was born in 1734. He was the son of a tavern-keeper farmer who lived in New London Township in Chester County, Pa. After studying for seven years at Rev. Francis Alison's academy at nearby New London, McKean read law with a cousin at New Castle, Del. In 1754 at age 20, he was admitted to the Delaware bar and soon expanded his practice into Pennsylvania and New Jersey.

During the next 25 years, McKean occupied appointive and elective offices in Delaware, some simultaneously: high sheriff of Kent County; militia captain; trustee of the loan office of New Castle County; customs collector and judge at New Castle; deputy attorney general of Sussex County; chief notary officer for the province; and clerk (1757-1759) and member (1762-1779) of the legislature, including the speakership of the lower house (1772-1773). In 1762, he had also helped compile the colony's laws.

McKean's Revolutionary tendencies had revealed themselves during the Stamp Act (1765) controversy. He was one of the most vociferous of the delegates at the Stamp Act Congress. In 1774, he established his home in Philadelphia. He retained membership in the Delaware legislature, which that same year elected him to the Continental Congress. Except for the period December 1776-January 1778, when conservative opposition unseated him, he stayed there until 1783 and served as president for a few months in 1781. He played a key role in the Revolutionary program, at the same time fostering the establishment of governments in Delaware and Pennsylvania.

From late 1776 until early in 1778, McKean had remained in the lower house of the Delaware legislature, of which he became speaker once again. In that capacity, in September-November 1777, he temporarily replaced the president of Delaware whom the British had captured. In vain they also pursued McKean, who was forced to move his family several times. Meantime, in July he had been appointed chief justice of the Pennsylvania Superior Court, a position he held for 22 years.

After 1783, his congressional service ended, and McKean focused his political activities in Pennsylvania. As a Federalist, in 1787 he was instrumental in that state's ratification of the U.S. Constitution. In the state constitutional convention of 1789-1790, he demonstrated mistrust of popular government. During the 1790s, disenchanted with Federalist foreign policy, he switched to the Democratic-Republicans.

While governor for three terms (1799-1808), McKean was the storm center of violent partisan warfare. Although he exercised strong leadership and advanced education and internal improvements, his imperiousness infuriated the Federalists, alienated many members of his own party, and resulted in an attempt to impeach him. Especially controversial were his rigid employment of the spoils system, including the appointment of friends and relatives, and his refusal to call a convention to revise the constitution. He won reelection only with the support of members of both parties who opposed the revision.

McKean lived out his life quietly in Philadelphia. He died in 1817 at age 83 and was buried in Laurel Hill Cemetery. His substantial estate consisted of stocks, bonds, and huge tracts of land in Pennsylvania.

ARTHUR MIDDLETON | SOUTH CAROLINA

Middleton was born in 1742 at Middleton Place, the family estate on the Ashley River near Charleston. His father, who owned a score of plantations comprising 50,000 acres and employing some 800 slaves, ranked among the wealthiest and most politically active men in the province. While still a young boy, Arthur sailed to England for an education. He attended Hackney School, graduated from Cambridge University, and studied law in London. In 1764, the year after his return, he embarked on a career as justice of the peace and colonial legislator. In 1768-1771, he and his wife made an extended tour of Europe.

Reelected the next year to the legislature, Middleton joined the Revolutionaries in their campaign against the Royal Governor. While sitting in the first and second provincial assemblies (1775-1776), Middleton aided in organizing a night raid on public arms stores at Charleston before the governor could seize them, raised money for armed resistance, recommended defense measures for Charleston Harbor, served on the council of safety, and urged tight enforcement of the Continental Association. An extremist, he advocated the tarring and feathering of Loyalists and confiscating the estates of those who had fled the country.

In 1776, Middleton was chosen to replace his more conservative father in the Continental Congress. Two years later, young Middleton declined reelection and rejected an offer of the governorship of South Carolina by the legislature, which had enacted a new constitution that he opposed. In 1779 and 1780, though reelected to the Continental Congress, Middleton failed to attend, probably because of concern over the British threat to his state. While serving in the militia during the siege of Charleston in 1780, he was captured by the British and imprisoned at St. Augustine, Fla., until July 1781.

Two months later, Middleton returned to Congress and served throughout 1782. He then retired to Middleton Place, which had been ravaged by the British, rehabilitated it, resumed his life as a planter, sat intermittently in the state legislature, and accepted assignment as one of the original trustees of the College of Charleston. He died in 1787 at age 44. His remains rest at Middleton Place.

The Battle of Lexington, April 1775.

Born in 1726, Morris was the son of the second lord of the vast manor of Morrisania in Westchester (present Bronx) County, N.Y. Upon graduating from Yale College in 1746, he helped manage the estate. In 1762, when his father died, he inherited Morrisania and became its third lord. About this time, he gained an interest in local politics and in 1769, served a term in the colonial legislature.

Though residing in a pro-Loyalist county, Morris became increasingly critical of British policy. In 1775, he helped organize a meeting at White Plains that overcame strong opposition and chose county delegates, including Morris as chairman, to New York's first provincial convention. It elected him to the Continental Congress (1775-1777), where he specialized in military and Indian affairs. For most of 1776, he was absent from Philadelphia, serving as a brigadier general in the Westchester County militia. During the British in-

vasion of New York that year, the redcoats ravaged Morrisania and forced Morris's family to flee.

When his career in Congress ended, Morris rose to the rank of major general in the militia and became a county judge (1777-1778) and state senator (1777-1781 and 1784-1788). After war's end in 1783, when he returned to Morrisania, he devoted much of his time to rehabilitating it. In 1784, he sat on the first board of regents of the University of New York. Four years later, at the state ratifying convention in Poughkeepsie, he strongly supported Alexander Hamilton's successful drive for approval of the U.S. Constitution.

Morris died in 1798 at Morrisania at age 71. His grave is in the family vault in St. Ann's Church in the Bronx.

Morris was born in or near Liverpool, England, in 1734. At age 13, he immigrated to Maryland to join his father, a tobacco exporter at Oxford, Md. After brief schooling at Philadelphia, the youth obtained employment with a well-known shipping firm. In 1754, he became a partner and for almost four decades was one of the company's directors as well as one of Philadelphia's most influential citizens.

During the Stamp Act turmoil in 1765, Morris had joined other merchants in protest, but not until the outbreak of hostilities a decade hence did he fully commit himself to the Revolution. In 1775, the Continental Congress contracted with his firm to import arms and ammunition, and he was elected to the Pennsylvania council of safety (1775-1776), the committee of correspondence, the provincial assembly (1775-1776), the state legislature (1776-1778), and the Continental Congress (1775-1778). On July 1, 1776, he voted against independence, which he considered premature, but the next day, was purposely absent to facilitate an affirmative ballot by his state.

Morris specialized in financial affairs and military procurement. Had it not been for his assiduous labors, the Continental Army would probably have demobilized. He worked closely with General Washington, wheedled money and supplies from the states, borrowed money in the face of overwhelming difficulties, and even obtained personal loans to further the war cause. Immediately following his congressional service, Morris sat for two more terms in the Pennsylvania legislature in 1778-1781. During this time, Thomas Paine and others attacked him for profiteering in Congress, which investigated and vindicated him. Nevertheless, his reputation slipped.

Morris accepted the office of superintendent of finance (1781-1784) under the Articles of Confederation. Congress granted him dictatorial powers and acquiesced to his condition that he be allowed to continue his commercial enterprises. He slashed all government and military expenditures, personally purchased army and navy supplies, tightened accounting procedures, prodded the states to fulfill quotas of money and supplies, and strained his personal credit by issuing notes over his own signature or borrowing from friends.

To finance Washington's Yorktown campaign in 1781, Morris also obtained a sizable loan from France. He used part of it, along with some of his own fortune, to organize the Bank of North America, chartered that December. The first government-incorporated bank in the United States, it aided war financing.

Although Morris was reelected to the Pennsylvania legislature in 1785-1786, his private commercial ventures consumed most of his time. In 1786, he attended the Annapolis Convention and the following year the Constitutional Convention, where he sympathized with the Federalists. In 1789, declining Washington's offer of appointment as the first secretary of the Treasury, he took a senatorial seat in Congress (1789-1795).

Later, in his public life, Morris speculated wildly, often on overextended credit, in lands in the West and at the site of Washington, D.C. In 1794, he began constructing on Philadelphia's Chestnut Street a palatial townhouse designed by Maj. Pierre Charles L'Enfant. Soon, Morris attempted to escape creditors by retreating to The Hills, the country estate along the Schuylkill River that he had acquired in 1770.

Arrested at the behest of creditors in 1798 and forced to abandon completion of the townhouse, known in its unfinished state as "Morris' Folly," Morris was thrown into the Philadelphia debtors' prison. By the time he was released in 1801 under a Federal bankruptcy law, his property and fortune had vanished, his health deteriorated, and his spirit had been broken. He lingered on amid poverty and obscurity, living in a simple Philadelphia home on an annuity his friend Gouverneur Morris had obtained for his wife. He died in 1806 at age 72 and was buried in the yard at Christ Church.

JOHN MORTON | PENNSYLVANIA

Morton was born of Finnish-Swedish descent in 1725 shortly after the death of his father, on a farm in Ridley Township, Chester (present Delaware) County. John Sketchley, an Englishman who subsequently married Morton's widowed mother, reared and educated him. Sketchley taught the boy the three Rs as well as surveying. Morton practiced that profession on and off all his life, as well as farming, politics, and jurisprudence.

At age 30, Morton entered politics. From 1756 until a few months before he died in 1777, he served 18 terms in the colonial/state legislature (1756-1766 and 1769-1776), which he presided over during the last year and a half. In 1774, he won appointment as an associate justice of the Pennsylvania Supreme Court.

Morton had always maintained strong ties with his own county. He resided there all his life, remained active in civic and church affairs, and stayed close to the people. Between terms of office as county justice of the peace (1757-1764 and 1770-1774), he worked as sheriff (1766-1769).

Morton's service to the nation began in 1765 while he was a member of the Pennsylvania legislature. He and two colleagues represented the colony at the Stamp Act Congress in New York. His most dramatic act as delegate to the Continental Congress (1774-1777), in which he numbered among the moderates, was his sudden and crucial switch on July 1, 1776, to the side of Benjamin Franklin and James Wilson in the vote for national independence. On the final vote the next day, these three ballots outweighed those of Thomas Willing and Charles Humphreys. Robert Morris and John Dickinson being purposely absent, Pennsylvania registered a "yea." Morton was a member of many committees, in 1777 chairing the committee of the whole on the adoption of the Articles of Confederation, finally ratified after his death.

In spring 1777, Morton fell ill and died on his farm at age 51. His grave is in Old St. Paul's Cemetery in Chester, Pa.

Illustration published by Benjamin Franklin, 1754.

Nelson was born at Yorktown, Va., in 1738. At age 14, he sailed to England to supplement his initial tutorial education. In 1761, after graduating from Hackney School and Cambridge University, he returned to Virginia to help his father manage his plantation and mercantile business.

In 1764, Nelson became a justice of the peace for York County and entered the House of Burgesses. He served in the house until May 1774, when Royal Governor Lord Dunmore, provoked at its protests over the Boston Port Act, dissolved it. That year and the next, Nelson attended three of the Virginia provincial assemblies, where he worked closely with Patrick Henry. The last assembly elected Nelson to the Continental Congress, at which time he resigned his colonelcy in the Virginia militia.

In Congress, Nelson was outspoken in his desire to sever the bonds with England. At a convention held in Williamsburg in May 1776, he introduced and won approval for a resolution recommending national independence. Nelson carried it to Philadelphia and presented it to Richard Henry Lee, who redrafted and condensed it into his June 7 resolution. Not long afterward, Nelson's health began to decline. Subsequently, he divided his time between Philadelphia and Virginia, and in spring 1777, resigned from Congress.

Back in Virginia, Nelson was awarded the rank of brigadier general in the militia and was elected to the lower house of the legislature. Nelson served in Congress for a short time in 1779, but poor health forced him to retire once more. Nevertheless, in 1780, he obtained munitions and supplies for the militia, commanded troops, attended the legislature, and raised money to help subsidize the war. He was particularly effective in soliciting funds from wealthy plantation owners, to whom he pledged to repay the loans personally if the state should fail to do so.

When the British invaded Virginia in 1780-1781, civilian control seriously hampered Nelson's effectiveness as a militia commander. Consequently, in the latter year the legislature elected him as governor and granted him powers approaching those of a military dictator. Although still bothered by ill health, he kept the government intact and strengthened defenses. In September-October 1781, while taking part in the Yorktown siege, according to family tradition, he ordered troops to shell his own mansion when he learned it was a British headquarters. Soon after the victory at Yorktown, overwhelmed by the burdens of office and still in poor physical condition, he resigned the governorship.

That same year, Nelson partially retired to Offley Hoo, a modest estate in Hanover County that his father had willed to him in 1772. In financial distress from his wartime sacrifices, the younger Nelson lacked money to renovate his Yorktown home, where he had lived since 1767. Except for occasional tours in the legislature and visits to Yorktown, he devoted the rest of his life to his business affairs. He died at Offley Hoo in 1789 at age 50. His grave is at Yorktown in Grace Episcopal Churchyard.

WILLIAM PACA | MARYLAND

The son of a prominent planter-landowner, Paca, probably of Italian descent, was born in 1740 at Chilbury Hall near Abingdon in Harford County, Md. He received his early education from private tutors and at age 15, matriculated at the College of Philadelphia (later part of the University of Pennsylvania). Upon graduating, he studied with an attorney in Annapolis and read law in London. In 1763, the year before initiating his practice in Annapolis, he began building a home, completed two years later. When in the country, he resided at Wye Plantation in Queen Anne's County, which he had purchased about 1760.

In 1768, Paca won a seat in the colonial legislature, where he soon aligned himself with Samuel Chase and other Whigs in protesting the powers of the proprietary governor. In the early 1770s, Paca joined other Maryland patriots in urging governmental regulation of fees paid to civil officers and in opposing the poll tax used to pay the salaries of Anglican clergy representing the established church. In 1773, he became a member of the Maryland committee of correspondence.

Although he sat in Congress until 1779, Paca's most noteworthy efforts were on the state level. In spring and early summer 1776, the provincial convention, a relatively conservative body, refused to authorize its congressional delegates to vote for independence. Paca drummed up enough support on the home front to persuade the convention to change its mind and bring Maryland into the affirmative column in the congressional voting July 1-2, 1776. A few months later, he helped draft a state constitution. The next year, he began a two-year term in the Maryland senate and saw militia duty. In addition, he sat on the council of safety and spent large amounts of his own money outfitting troops.

Between 1778 and 1782, Paca distinguished himself first as chief justice of the state Superior Court and then as chief judge of the circuit court of appeals in admiralty and prize cases. In 1780, he sold his home in Annapolis and moved permanently to Wye Plantation. In 1782, he raised funds for Washington College, founded that same year in Chestertown as the first institution of higher learning in Maryland, and served on the board of visitors. As governor of Maryland (1782-1785), he concerned himself with the welfare of war veterans and other postwar problems.

A delegate to the state convention to ratify the Federal Constitution in 1788, Paca urged its adoption, if amended, and helped draw up a list of proposed amendments. In 1789, President Washington appointed him as federal district judge. He held this position until 1799, the year of his death at age 58, at Wye Hall on Wye Island. At first interred at Wye Hall, Paca's remains now rest in the family burial ground near Wye Plantation.

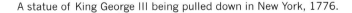

A statue of King George III being pulled down in New York, 1776.

Paine was born at Boston in 1731. His father was a merchant who had once been a clergyman. Young Paine led his class at Boston Latin School and graduated from Harvard in 1749. He taught school for a time before yielding to family tradition and entering the ministry.

In 1755, during the French and Indian War, he served as chaplain on a military expedition to Crown Point, N.Y. To improve his health, he made a voyage to the Carolinas, England, Spain, and Greenland. He decided to forsake the ministry for the law and was admitted to the Massachusetts bar in 1757. He opened an office in Portland but in 1761, moved to Taunton.

Paine early became involved in the patriot movement. He was chosen in 1770 as one of the prosecuting attorneys in the Boston Massacre trial and thus gained recognition throughout the Colonies. Between 1773 and 1778, except in 1776, he served in the Massachusetts legislature, in 1777 being speaker of the lower house. He was one of the first five delegates sent by Massachusetts to the Continental Congress (1774-1776), where he specialized in military and Indian affairs.

Although reelected to Congress in 1777, Paine chose to stay in Massachusetts. In addition to his legislative speakership, he was elected as the first attorney general, a position he held until 1790. Between 1778 and 1780, he played a prominent role in drafting the Massachusetts constitution. From 1790 until 1804, he sat as an associate justice of the Superior Court.

Meantime, in 1780, Paine moved from Taunton to Boston and had become active in civic affairs. That same year he was one of the founders of the American Academy of Arts and Sciences. Politically, he aligned himself with the Federalists. In 1804, increasing deafness brought about his retirement from the Superior Court, and he died a decade later at age 83 in Boston. He was buried in the Old Granary Burying Ground.

Penn was born in 1740 or 1741 in Caroline County, Va., the son of a well-to-do farmer. Despite the family's social position, Penn received only a few years of formal schooling. At age 18 when his father died, he inherited a sizable estate. But he was dissatisfied with the prospects it offered and decided to continue his education. Encouraged by a relative, Edmund Pendleton, a well-known lawyer who made available his personal library, Penn studied law on his own and within three years gained admittance to the bar.

In 1774, at the end of more than a decade of successful law practice in Virginia, Penn journeyed to Granville County, N.C., and made his home near Stovall. In 1775, he was elected to the provincial assembly and only a few weeks later to the Continental Congress (1775-1780). In 1777, he inherited the leadership of his state's delegation. He was one of the 16 signers of the Declaration who also signed the Articles of Confederation.

Remarkably efficient, likeable, and discreet, Penn quickly won the respect of his congressional colleagues. He rarely disputed with others but when he did, his good humor and peaceful manner saved the day.

Late in 1780, the governor of North Carolina recalled Penn from Congress to sit on the emergency Board of War, created by the legislature in September to share with the governor responsibility for military affairs. The three-man board, of which Penn became the leading member, in effect soon assumed control of all military matters. The governor and military officials, resenting the infringement upon their prerogatives and their loss of authority, persuaded the legislature to abolish the board in January 1781.

His health declining, the following July Penn declined an appointment to the Governor's Council. Except for a short tour in 1784 as state tax receiver for the Confederation, he apparently devoted his last years to his law practice. In 1788, in his late forties, he died at his home near Stovall. Originally buried in the family graveyard adjacent to his home, his remains now rest in Guilford Courthouse National Military Park in Greensboro.

<hr />

GEORGE READ | DELAWARE

Read's Dublin-born father was a landholder of means. Soon after Read's birth in 1733 in Cecil County, Md., his family moved to New Castle, Del., where the youth grew up. He attended school at Chester, Pa., and Rev. Francis Alison's academy at New London, Pa. At about age 15, he began reading law with a Philadelphia lawyer. In 1753, he was admitted to the bar and began to practice. The next year, he journeyed back to New Castle, hung out his shingle, and enlisted a clientele that extended into Maryland.

While crown attorney general (1763-1774) for the Three Lower Counties (present Delaware), Read protested against the Stamp Act. In 1765, he began a career in the colonial legislature that lasted more than a decade. A moderate Whig, he supported nonimportation measures and dignified protests. His attendance in Congress (1774-1777) was irregular. He was willing to protect colonial rights but was wary of extremism. He balloted against independence on July 2, 1776, either bowing to the strong Tory sentiment in Delaware or believing reconciliation with Britain was still possible.

That same year, Read gave priority to state responsibilities. He presided over the Delaware constitutional convention, in which he chaired the drafting committee and began a term as speaker of the legislative council, which in effect made him vice president of the state. When the British captured Wilmington the next fall, they captured the president, a resident of the city. At first, because Read was away in Congress, Thomas McKean, speaker of the lower house, took over as acting president. But in November, after almost being captured while he and his family were en route to Dover from Philadelphia, newly captured by the British, Read assumed the office and held it until spring 1778.

During 1779, in poor health, Read resigned from the legislative council, refused reelection to Congress, and began a period of inactivity. In 1782-1788, he again sat on the council and concurrently held the position of judge of the court of appeals in admiralty cases. Meantime, in 1784, he had served on a commission that adjusted New York-Massachusetts land claims. In 1786, he attended the Annapolis Convention. The next year, he participated in the Constitutional Convention. He later led the ratification movement in Delaware, the first state to ratify.

In the U.S. Senate (1789-1793), Read's attendance was again sporadic, but when present he allied with the Federalists. He resigned to accept the post of chief justice of Delaware. He held this office until his death at New Castle five years later, just three days after his 65th birthday. His grave is there in the Immanuel Episcopal Churchyard.

CAESAR RODNEY | DELAWARE

R odney was born in 1728 on his father's 800-acre plantation, Byfield, near Dover in Kent County. In 1745, he inherited the plantation. Despite a lack of formal and legal education, a decade later he accepted the first of a series of county offices: high sheriff, register of wills, recorder of deeds, clerk of the orphans' court, justice of the peace, militia captain, and cotrustee of the loan office.

On the provincial level, for most of 1758-1776, Rodney functioned as a justice of the Superior Court for the Three Lower Counties (present Delaware) and as a legislator in the lower house, including many tours as speaker. Between 1765 and 1774, he owned and occupied a townhouse that he used while in Dover. He and Thomas McKean compiled the colony's laws, and they both attended the Stamp Act Congress (1765). Three years later, they and George Read drafted a protest to the king concerning the Townshend Acts. In 1774, after Parliament closed Boston Harbor, Rodney usurped the prerogative of the proprietary governor by calling a special meeting of the legislature at New Castle, the first Revolutionary convention in the state. Rodney, McKean, and Read were sent to the First Continental Congress.

Although a congressional member for two years, Rodney was often absent in Delaware, sometimes presiding over the legislature and sometimes meeting military responsibilities. In May 1775, he was elected a colonel in the militia and in September, to brigadier general. Late the next June, while the independence resolution was pending in Congress, he was investigating Loyalist agitations in Sussex County. On the evening of July 1, after his return to Byfield, he received McKean's dispatch pointing out that Read had voted against independence that day and pleading with Rodney to hurry to Philadelphia to break the tie. Riding all night through a thunderstorm and stopping only to change horses, he completed the 80-mile trip just in time to make possible an affirmative vote for Delaware.

This brought down the wrath of the Kent County conservatives on Rodney, who was not reelected to Congress or to the legislature and not appointed to the state constitutional convention. He turned to military affairs, recruiting troops and taking part in minor actions in Delaware and New Jersey. In September 1777, acting State President McKean commissioned him as a major general.

That spring, the legislature had designated Rodney as an admiralty judge. In December, it reelected him to the Continental Congress. The next year, it nominated him as state president (1778-1781), in which capacity he stimulated the Delaware war effort. When he left office, he belatedly sought medical treatment in Philadelphia for a cancerous growth on his face, which had been bothering him for a decade and which he had covered with a green silk veil. In 1783, he entered the state senate and accepted the speakership, but passed away the next year at age 55. Interred originally at Byfield Plantation, his remains are now buried in Christ Episcopal Church Cemetery in Dover.

The son of an Anglican clergyman who had emigrated from Scotland, Ross was born in 1730 at New Castle, Del. After a preliminary classical education, he read law with his stepbrother, John, at Philadelphia and in 1750, entered the bar. Settling the next year at Lancaster, Pa., he built up a successful law practice and served as crown prosecutor for Cumberland County (1751-1763). A member of the colonial legislature from 1768 until 1775, he sometimes joined in its disputes with the proprietary governor and demonstrated an interest in Indian affairs.

Meantime, in 1774, despite his Loyalist leanings, a provincial convention to which Ross had been elected sent him to the Continental Congress. The next year, by which time he had for some reason decided to affiliate with the Revolutionaries, he also served on the Pennsylvania council of safety and held a military colonelcy. In 1776, he assisted in negotiating a peace treaty with the Indians in northwestern Pennsylvania and acted as vice president of the state constitutional convention, for which he helped draft a declaration of rights. Not a member of Congress during the voting for independence on July 1-2, 1776, he received his appointment soon enough to sign the Declaration on August 2. Illness brought about his resignation in January 1777.

In 1778, while Ross was acting as admiralty judge in Pennsylvania, a congressional court of appeals overruled his decision in a case involving a dispute between a citizen of Connecticut and the State of Pennsylvania. Ross, refusing to acknowledge the authority of the higher court to counter state decisions, initiated a dispute between Pennsylvania and the central government that represented an early manifestation of the states' rights controversy and did not subside until 1809. But Ross did not live to see the outcome, for he died in Philadelphia in 1779 at age 49. He was buried in Christ Church Burial Ground.

Rush was born in 1745 at Byberry ("The Homestead"), near Philadelphia. When Rush was five, his farmer-gunsmith father died. The youth obtained a sound education at West Nottingham Academy in Rising Sun, Md., and graduated from the College of New Jersey (later Princeton University). Returning to Philadelphia in 1760, he apparently first considered studying law but chose medicine. In 1766, after a five-year apprenticeship to a local physician, he sailed to Scotland where two years later the University of Edinburgh awarded him a medical degree.

In 1769, after further training in London, he came back to Philadelphia and set up practice. Before the year was out, he obtained the first professorship of chemistry in the country at the College of Philadelphia and wrote the first American textbook on the subject.

Rush's tour in the Continental Congress was brief. In June 1776, he attended a Pennsylvania conference of patriots and helped draft a declaration of the colony's support for national independence. In recognition of these services, the following month the provincial convention sent him to Congress—after the adoption of the Declaration. In December, Philadelphia threatened by British invasion, the government fled to Baltimore. Rush apparently did not spend much time there. That same month, he took part in General Washington's New Jersey campaign as a surgeon in the Philadelphia militia.

In April 1777, Rush accepted the position of surgeon general in the Middle Department of the Continental Army. Abhorring the deplorable conditions prevailing in the medical service, in a complaint to Washington he accused his superior, Dr. William Shippen, of maladministration. Washington referred the matter to Congress, which vindicated Shippen. In January 1778, Rush angrily resigned. His subsequent criticisms of Washington and his participation in the Conway Cabal, a movement to replace General Washington, ended his military and, for a time, his political career. He resumed his medical practice in Philadelphia.

In 1787, Rush wrote tracts in the newspapers endorsing the U.S. Constitution. In the Commonwealth ratifying convention that same year, he aided James Wilson in the struggle for its adoption. In 1789-1790, Rush attended the Pennsylvania constitutional convention. From 1797 until 1813, he served as treasurer of the U.S. Mint.

Rush, through his writings and lectures, had become probably the best-known physician and medical teacher in the land, and he fostered Philadelphia's ascendancy as the early medical center of the nation. His students came from as far away as Europe to attend his classes at the College of Philadelphia and its successors, the University of the State of Pennsylvania and the University of Pennsylvania (1791). He served on the staff of the Pennsylvania Hospital from 1783 until the end of his life, helped found the Philadelphia College of Physicians (1787), and held office as first president of the Philadelphia Medical Society. In 1786, he founded the Philadelphia Dispensary, the first free medical clinic in the country. His work among the insane at the Pennsylvania Hospital resulted in *Medical Inquiries and Observations Upon the Diseases of the Mind* (1812), which to some degree foreshadowed modern psychiatric techniques.

Although he was one of the few doctors who remained in Philadelphia during the devastating yellow fever epidemics of 1793 and 1798, his opponents criticized his methods of treatment.

Aroused by the idealism of the Revolution and the plight of the poor and sick he encountered in his medical practice, Rush helped pioneer various humanitarian and social movements that were to restructure U.S. life in the 19th century. These included abolition of slavery and educational and prison reform. Rush also condemned public and capital punishment and advocated temperance. Many of his reform articles appeared in *Essays: Literary, Moral, and Philosophical* (1798).

Finally, Rush helped organize and sat as a trustee of Dickinson College (1783), aided in founding the Pennsylvania Society for Promoting the Abolition of Slavery (1787) and later served as its president, enjoyed membership in the American Philosophical Society, and was a cofounder and vice president of the Philadelphia Bible Society, which advocated the use of scripture in the public schools.

A typhus epidemic claimed Rush's life at age 67 in 1813. His grave is in Christ Church Burial Ground in Philadelphia.

The child of an Irish immigrant and physician, Rutledge was born in 1749 at or near Charleston, S.C. As a young man he studied law in England. In 1773, during his first year of practice on his return to Charleston, he won Whig acclaim by obtaining the release of newspaper publisher Thomas Powell, who had been imprisoned by the Crown for printing an article critical of the Loyalist upper house of the colonial legislature. The next year, the grateful Whigs named Rutledge as one of five delegates to the First Continental Congress.

Rutledge spent his first congressional term in the shadow of the more experienced South Carolina delegates. During 1775-1776, however, both in Congress and in two South Carolina provincial assemblies, his increasing self-confidence and maturation of judgment brought him the esteem of his associates. In 1776, Rutledge, found himself the delegation leader.

On June 7, 1776, when Richard Henry Lee of Virginia proposed national independence, Rutledge led the moderates in securing a delay in the voting. He knew that independence was inevitable. In March, his colony had adopted a constitution and the provincial assembly had empowered its delegates to vote for independence if they so desired. Yet Rutledge firmly believed the Colonies should first confederate and nurture foreign alliances to strengthen themselves for the perilous step they were about to take. When the vote on independence came up on July 1, he refused to yield, and South Carolina balloted negatively. But nine of the Colonies voted affirmatively. Rutledge, realizing that the resolution would probably carry anyway, proposed that the vote be recast the following day. He persuaded the other South Carolina delegates to submit to the will of the majority for the sake of unanimity, and South Carolina reversed its position.

Rutledge in September accompanied John Adams and Benjamin Franklin on a vain peace mission to Staten Island to negotiate with British Admiral Lord Richard Howe, who with his brother, Gen. William Howe, was trying to resolve the differences between the Colonies and the mother country. Two months later, Rutledge departed from Congress to resume his law practice in Charleston.

In 1778, Rutledge accepted a seat in the state legislature and in 1779 won reelection to Congress, though military duties prevented his attendance. As a militia captain, in February 1779, he took part in Gen. William Moultrie's defeat of the British at Port Royal Island, S.C. But in May 1780, during the siege of Charleston, the redcoats captured Rutledge and imprisoned him at St. Augustine, Fla., until July 1781.

From 1782 until 1798, Rutledge sat in the state legislature, which on three occasions designated him as a presidential elector. During this period, his mistrust of unbridled republicanism reinforced his conservatism and brought him into the Federalist Party. In private life he flourished, his wealth increasing through his law practice and investments in plantations. In 1798, he was elected governor of South Carolina. But, his health poor, he died at Charleston early in 1800 at age 50, nearly a year before the end of his term. St. Philip's Episcopal Church Cemetery is the site of his grave.

ROGER SHERMAN | CONNECTICUT

In 1723, when Sherman was two years old, his family relocated from his Newton, Mass., birthplace to Dorchester (present Stoughton). As a boy, he was spurred by a desire to learn and read widely in his spare time to supplement his minimal education at a common school. But he spent most of his waking hours helping his father with farming chores and learning the cobbler's trade from him. In 1743, two years after his father's death, Sherman joined an older brother who had settled at New Milford, Conn.

Purchasing a store, becoming county surveyor, and winning a variety of town offices, Sherman prospered and assumed leadership in the community. Without benefit of a legal education, he was admitted to the bar in 1754 and embarked upon a distinguished judicial and political career. In 1755-1761, except for a brief interval, he served as a representative in the colonial legislature and held the offices of justice of the peace and county judge. He also published an essay on monetary theory and a series of almanacs incorporating his own astronomical observations and verse.

In 1761, abandoning his law practice, Sherman moved to New Haven, Conn., and managed a store that catered to Yale students and another one in nearby Wallingford. He also became a friend and benefactor of Yale College and for many years was its treasurer.

Meanwhile, Sherman rose from justice of the peace and county judge to an associate judge of the Connecticut Superior Court and to representative in both houses of the colonial assembly. Although opposed to extremism, he early joined the fight against Britain. He supported nonimportation measures and headed the New Haven committee of correspondence.

Sherman was a longtime and influential member of the Continental Congress (1774-1781 and 1783-1784). He won membership on the committees that drafted the Declaration of Independence and the Articles of Confederation and those concerned with Indian affairs, national finance, and military matters. To solve economic problems at national and state levels, he advocated high taxes rather than excessive borrowing or the issuance of paper currency. While in Congress, Sherman remained active in state and local politics, continuing to hold the office of judge of the Connecticut Superior Court and membership on the council of safety. In 1783, he helped codify Connecticut's statutory laws and was elected mayor of New Haven (1784-1786).

In 1787, Sherman represented his state at the Constitutional Convention. He conceived and introduced the Connecticut, or so-called Great, Compromise, which broke a deadlock between the large and small states by providing for a dual legislative system—representation by proportion of population in the lower house and equal representation in the upper house. He also was instrumental in Connecticut's ratification of the Constitution.

Sherman capped his career by serving as U.S. representative (1789-1791) and senator (1791-1793), espousing the Federalist cause. He died at New Haven in 1793 at age 72 and is buried in the Grove Street Cemetery.

Smith was born in northern Ireland about 1719. When he was around 10, his father immigrated to America and settled west of the Susquehanna River in York County, Pa. James studied surveying and classical languages and then read law in the office of his older brother at Lancaster. He was admitted to the bar in 1745 and moved westward to the Shippensburg vicinity in Cumberland County. A lack of clients and surveying work caused him about 1750 to relocate eastward to York. Although he was the only lawyer in town until 1769, he experienced difficulty in recruiting clients. Probably for this reason: during 1771-1778, he undertook iron manufacturing, but the venture failed and he lost £5,000.

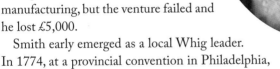

Smith early emerged as a local Whig leader. In 1774, at a provincial convention in Philadelphia, he supported nonimportation measures and advocated an intercolonial congress. At York he raised a militia company where he served as captain and then honorary colonel. At two provincial meetings in 1775-1776, he championed the interests of the western counties and helped formulate resolutions calling for independence, the strengthening of defenses, and establishment of a new provincial government. During the latter year, he sat on the drafting committee in the state constitutional convention. Elected to Congress (1776-1778) on July 20, 1776, he arrived in Philadelphia in time to sign the Declaration.

During 1779-1782, Smith held various state offices: one-term legislator, judge of the Pennsylvania high court of errors and appeals, brigadier general in the militia, and state counselor during the Wyoming Valley land dispute between Pennsylvania and Connecticut. In 1785, he turned down reelection to Congress because of his age. His major activity prior to his 1801 retirement was the practice of law. Smith died at about age 87 in 1806 at York. His grave is in the First Presbyterian Church Cemetery.

Stockton, son of a wealthy landowner and judge, was born in 1730 at Morven, the family estate and his lifelong home, at Princeton, N.J. After a preparatory education at West Nottingham Academy in Rising Sun, Md., he graduated in 1748 from the College of New Jersey (later Princeton University). In 1754, he completed an apprenticeship with a Newark lawyer and joined the bar. By the mid-1760s, he was recognized as one of the ablest lawyers in the Middle Colonies. In 1768, he began a six-year term on the executive council of New Jersey and then sat on the provincial Supreme Court (1774-1776).

Stockton became associated with the Revolutionary movement during its initial stages. In 1764, he advocated American representation in Parliament, but during the Stamp Act crisis the next year questioned its right to control the Colonies at all. By 1774, he was espousing colonial self-rule under the Crown. Elected to Congress two years later, he voted for independence and signed the Declaration. That same year, he met defeat in a bid for the New Jersey governorship but rejected the chance to become first chief justice of the State Supreme Court to remain in Congress.

Late in 1776, while inspecting the northern Continental Army in upper New York State with fellow Congressman George Clymer, Stockton hurried home when he learned of the British invasion of New Jersey and removed his family to a friend's home in Monmouth County. While he was there, Loyalists informed the British, who captured and imprisoned him under harsh conditions at Perth Amboy, N.J., and later in New York. A formal remonstrance from Congress and other efforts to obtain his exchange resulted in his release, in poor physical condition, sometime in 1777. To add to his woes, he found that the British had pillaged and partially burned Morven. Still an invalid, Stockton died at Princeton in 1781 at age 50. He is buried at the Stony Brook Quaker Meeting House Cemetery.

Stone was born in 1743 at Poynton Manor, his father's plantation near the village of Welcome in Charles County, Md., and enjoyed all the advantages as the eldest son. Following tutorial instruction in the classics as a youth, he apprenticed himself to an Annapolis lawyer and in 1764, joined the bar. For the first two years he practiced at Frederick, Md., and then settled in his home county. He purchased land a few miles to the northeast of his birthplace. There, near Port Tobacco, in 1771 he built Habre-de-Venture, his home and principal residence for the rest of his life.

Stone entered politics in 1773 as a member of the Charles County committee of correspondence. In 1774, on behalf of the proprietary governor, he helped prosecute Joseph H. Harrison, a Maryland legislator who had refused to pay the poll tax for the support of the Anglican clergy. This action, despite its legal ethicality, did not endear Stone to the patriots.

That same year, Stone won appointment to the provincial convention, which sent him to Congress in 1775. He heartily favored reconciliation almost up to the time of the vote on independence and was one of the few delegates who favored peace negotiations with Britisher Lord Richard Howe in September 1776, some two months after the adoption of the Declaration. Stone rarely participated in debates but sat on the committee that drafted the Articles of Confederation, though he did not sign the document. He remained in Congress until 1778.

Meantime, a couple of years earlier, Stone had begun a tour in the state senate that was to last for almost the remainder of his life. In 1784, he returned to the Continental Congress, where he served for a few days as acting president but resigned before the year expired to resume his law practice. His last act of public service occurred in 1785, when he and two others represented Maryland at the Mount Vernon Conference.

In 1787, Stone's wife passed away at age 34. The grief-stricken Stone abandoned his work, declined to attend the Constitutional Convention to which he had been elected, and decided to visit England. A few months later, though only in his mid-forties, he died suddenly at Alexandria, Va. Stone is buried in the family graveyard adjacent to Habre-de-Venture.

<hr />

GEORGE TAYLOR | PENNSYLVANIA

When Taylor was about 20, he indentured himself and emigrated from Northern Ireland, where he had been born in 1716, to Pennsylvania. He began as a laborer and then became clerk at Warwick Furnace in Chester County. Within three years, he rose to bookkeeper-manager of nearby Coventry Forge, another enterprise of his employer. In 1742, the year after the latter died, Taylor acquired his business when he married his widow.

In the mid-1750s, Taylor moved to Bucks County, where he and a partner leased Durham Furnace, about two miles south of the Northampton County line and 10 miles south of Easton. Apparently after 1763, Taylor lived much of the time at or near Easton and acquired property there. In 1768, he built a home west of the city on a 331-acre tract he had purchased the year before. In 1771, he leased most of the land out as a farm and five years later sold the house and land.

Taylor had begun his public life in 1747, when he took a commission as a captain in the Chester County militia. In 1761, he was appointed justice of the peace for Bucks County but devoted most of his energies to Northampton County, which he served as justice of the peace (1764-1775) and representative in the colonial legislature (1764-1770). In 1774, Taylor, a political moderate, became a member of the Northampton County committee of correspondence. The next year, he attended a provincial Revolutionary convention, was elected to the provincial assembly, served on the council of safety, and became a colonel in the Bucks and Northampton County militias.

In July 1776, the Pennsylvania assembly selected Taylor as one of its new delegates to the Continental Congress. His only noteworthy action there was signing the Declaration. In March 1777, the voters of Northampton County elected Taylor to the new Supreme Executive Assembly of Pennsylvania, but illness and financial difficulties restricted his participation to only six weeks.

By this time, Taylor's Durham Furnace was turning out grapeshot, cannonballs, bar shot, and cannon for the Revolutionary army—for which Taylor was ill-compensated. In 1778, the state dispossessed him of his lease on the Durham Furnace. Taylor then moved to Greenwich Township, N.J., and leased Greenwich Forge, which he operated until his death at age 65 in 1781. The year before, his health failing, Taylor had returned to Easton and leased a home. Originally buried in the yard of the German Evangelical Lutheran Church of Easton, his body was later moved to the Easton Cemetery.

MATTHEW THORNTON | NEW HAMPSHIRE

Thornton was born in Ireland about 1714. Approximately four years later, his Scottish-Irish parents immigrated with their family to America, settling first at Wiscasset in present Maine, and then near Worcester, Mass. Young Thornton undertook the study of medicine with a local doctor. In 1740, he began what proved to be a thriving practice in the Scottish-Irish town of Londonderry (present Derry Village), N.H. Five years later, as a surgeon in the New Hampshire militia during King George's War (1740-1748), he participated in the British expedition from New England that captured Louisbourg, the French fortress in Nova Scotia.

By 1758, Thornton was representing Londonderry in the colonial legislature and stayed there until 1775. About 1760, he married and began a family; throughout the period he figured prominently in New Hampshire politics and Revolutionary activities. In 1775-1776, he held the office of president of the provincial assembly and constitutional convention, chairman of the council of safety, and member of the upper and lower houses of the legislature, and speaker of the former. Although he did not enter Congress until November 1776, three months after the formal signing of the Declaration, he was granted permission to affix his signature.

About a year later, Thornton left Congress to devote his time to his duties as associate justice of the state Superior Court. He had acquired this position in 1776 and held it until 1782, some two years after he retired from his medical practice in Londonderry and settled on a farm he purchased near Merrimack, N.H. In 1784-1786, he completed a tour in the state senate. He spent his last years farming and operating a ferry—Lutwyche's (later Thornton's) Ferry—across the Merrimack River.

Thornton died in 1803 at about age 89. His grave is in Thornton's Ferry Cemetery, near the site of his Merrimack home.

GEORGE WALTON | GEORGIA

Born in the 1740s near Farmville, Va., Walton was orphaned early and was reared by an uncle who apprenticed him to a carpenter. Walton supplemented extensive independent study with some formal schooling. In 1769, he moved to Savannah, Ga., read law under a local attorney, and five years later joined the bar.

That same year, Walton plunged into politics. Rallying Revolutionaries at Savannah, Walton helped organize and played a key part in meetings at Savannah in July and August 1774 and the first provincial congress the next January. But these meetings hardly set the dissent in motion. The divided delegates, aware of their limited constituency, failed to send delegates to the Continental Congress and thus alienated St. John's Parish. Except for creation of a committee of correspondence, to which Walton was appointed, the conferees for the most part substituted patriotic talk for action.

By July 1775, when the second provincial congress convened and designated Walton as secretary, apathy in the Revolutionary ranks had given way to aggressiveness. The congress dispatched four delegates to the Continental Congress to join Lyman Hall, already an unofficial "delegate" from St. John's Parish. The next year, the third provincial congress elected Walton, by this time chairman of the council of safety, as a delegate (1776-1781). In this capacity, he sat on committees dealing with western lands, national finance, and Indian affairs. His only lapse in attendance occurred in 1778-1779, when the military defense of his own state took precedence over his congressional obligations. As a colonel in the Georgia militia, he was wounded and captured during the siege of Savannah in November-December 1778— the beginning of the British invasion of the South. He was imprisoned until September 1779 when he was exchanged for a navy captain.

Right after his release, at Augusta Walton became involved in a factional dispute between two groups of Revolutionaries. Walton's group, irritated because their conservative opponents had taken advantage of the confusion generated by the British occupation of Savannah by putting their own "governor" into office without benefit of a general election, countered by selecting Walton as its "governor" (November 1779-January 1780). In January, the new legally elected legislature picked a governor, another anticonservative. Walton returned to the Continental Congress in 1780-1781, after which he returned to Georgia.

Walton's offices included those of chief justice (1783-1789) and justice (1790-1795 and 1799-1804) of the state Superior Court; delegate to the state constitutional convention (1788); presidential elector (1789); governor (1789-1790); and U.S. senator (1795-1796), filling out an unexpired term. Meantime, he had been elected as a delegate to the U.S. Constitutional Convention (1787), but did not attend. He was also a trustee and founder of Richmond Academy in Augusta and Franklin College (later the University of Georgia) in Athens.

About 1790, while governor, changing his residence from Savannah to the capital of Augusta, Walton built a cottage on the northern edge of the city on confiscated Loyalist lands he had acquired. He lived in the cottage for five years and then moved to College Hill, a country estate he erected on the western outskirts. He died there in 1804. Assigned first to the Rosney Cemetery in Augusta, his remains now rest at the Signers' Monument in that city.

Whipple was born in 1730 at Kittery in present Maine. He attended local schools and went to sea while still a boy. In his early twenties he became a shipmaster, and later, probably sometimes engaged in the slave trade. About 1760, he gave up the sea and founded a mercantile firm at Portsmouth, N.H., with his brother Joseph.

By the outbreak of the Revolution, Whipple had become one of the leading citizens of Portsmouth. In 1775, he left business to devote his time to public affairs and represented Portsmouth in the provincial assembly at Exeter and served on the New Hampshire council of safety. In 1776, he won seats in the upper house of the state legislature and in the Continental Congress. His congressional tour, interrupted intermittently by militia duty, lasted until 1779. He concerned himself mainly with military, marine, and financial matters. A tough-minded, independent individual, he recommended military aggressiveness in the war instead of diplomacy and favored severe punishment of Loyalists and speculators.

In fall 1777, Whipple, a brigadier general in the New Hampshire militia, led four regiments to upper New York State and helped encircle and besiege the British army at Saratoga. He was present on October 17 at the surrender of Gen. John Burgoyne; signed the Convention of Saratoga ending the New York campaign; and helped escort the British troops to a winter encampment near Boston to await embarkation for England. In 1778, he led another contingent of New Hampshire militia into Rhode Island on a campaign that sought but failed to recapture Newport from the British.

During his last years, Whipple held the offices of state legislator (1780-1784), associate justice of the New Hampshire Superior Court (1782-1785), receiver of finances for Congress in New Hampshire (1782-1784), and in 1782, president of a commission that arbitrated the Wyoming Valley land dispute between Connecticut and Pennsylvania. Ill the remaining few years of his life, he died in 1785 at age 55 at Portsmouth, where he was buried in Union Cemetery.

A Congregational pastor's son, Williams was born in 1731 at Lebanon, Conn., his lifelong home. After graduating from Harvard in 1751, he began studying for the ministry under his father. Four years later, during the French and Indian War (1754-1763), he accompanied a British expedition to Lake George, in northeastern New York, that won a victory. Back home, he became a merchant.

During his long political career, Williams held a myriad of local, provincial, and state offices: town clerk (1752-1796) and selectman (1760-1785); member, clerk, and speaker of the lower house of the colonial legislature (1755-1776); state legislator (1781-1784); member of the governor's council (1784-1803); judge of the Windham County court (1776-1805); and probate judge for the Windham district (1775-1809). He also represented Connecticut at New England meetings and attended the 1788 convention that ratified the Federal Constitution, of which he approved.

Upon the outbreak of the Revolution, Williams threw his weight behind the cause. Besides writing tracts for the press expressing the colonial viewpoint, he prepared Revolutionary state papers for Governor Trumbull. Williams also raised money for and personally contributed to the war effort. Between 1773 and 1776, he held a colonelcy in the Connecticut militia and served on the provincial council of safety. In Congress (1776-1778 and 1783-1784), he sat on the Board of War and helped frame the Articles of Confederation, though he did not sign them. During the winter of 1780-1781, while a French regiment was stationed in Lebanon, he moved out of his home and turned it over to the officers.

Williams died at age 80 in 1811. His grave is in the Trumbull Cemetery in Lebanon.

Wilson was born in 1741 or 1742 at Carskerdo, near St. Andrews, Scotland, and educated at the universities of St. Andrews, Glasgow, and Edinburgh. He immigrated to America, arriving in the midst of the Stamp Act agitations in 1765. Early the next year, he accepted a position as Latin tutor at the College of Philadelphia but abandoned it to study law under John Dickinson.

In 1768, the year after his admission to the bar, Wilson set up practice at Reading, Pa. Two years later, he moved westward to the Scottish-Irish settlement of Carlisle. He specialized in land law and built a broad clientele. On borrowed capital, he began to speculate in land. He also lectured for many years on English literature at the College of Philadelphia.

Wilson became involved in Revolutionary politics. In 1774, he took over chairmanship of the Carlisle committee of correspondence, attended the first provincial assembly, and completed preparation of "Considerations on the Nature and Extent of the Legislative Authority of the British Parliament." This tract circulated widely in England and America and established Wilson as a Whig leader. It denied Parliament's authority over the Colonies, though it did not question their allegiance to the Crown, and recommended a reorganization of the imperial structure similar to the later British Commonwealth of Nations.

In 1775, Wilson was elected to the provincial assembly and the Continental Congress, where he sat mainly on military and Indian affairs committees. In 1776, he joined the moderates in voting for a three-week delay in considering Richard Henry Lee's resolution of June 7. On July 1, however, Wilson dissented from the majority of the Pennsylvania delegation and balloted with John Morton and Benjamin Franklin for independence. On July 2, the three men, representing a majority of the commonwealth's delegates present, voted the same. Wilson's strenuous opposition to the Republican Pennsylvania Constitution of 1776, besides indicating his switch to conservatism, led to his removal from Congress the following year. He repaired to Annapolis during winter 1777-1778 and then resided in Philadelphia.

Wilson affirmed his newly assumed political stance by closely identifying with the aristocratic and conservative Republican groups, multiplying his business interests, and accelerating his land speculation. He also took a position as advocate-general for France in America (1779-1783), dealing with commercial and maritime matters, and legally defended Loyalists and their sympathizers.

In fall 1779, during a period of inflation and food shortages, a mob, including many militiamen and led by radical-constitutionalists, set out to attack the Republican leadership. Wilson was a prime target. He and some 35 of his colleagues barricaded themselves in his home at Third and Walnut Streets, henceforth known as "Fort Wilson." During a brief skirmish, several people on both sides were killed or wounded. The shock cooled sentiments, and pardons were issued all around, though major political battles over the commonwealth constitution still lay ahead.

During 1781, Congress appointed Wilson as one of the directors of the Bank of North America, newly founded by Robert Morris with the legal advice of Wilson. In 1782-1783, by which time the conservatives had regained some of their power, he was reelected to Congress, as well as in the period 1785-1787.

Wilson reached the apex of his career in the U.S. Constitutional Convention (1787), in which he was one of the leaders, both in the floor debates and the drafting committee. That same year, he led the drive for ratification in Pennsylvania, the second state to ratify. The new commonwealth constitution, drafted in 1789-1790 along the lines of the U.S. Constitution, was primarily Wilson's work and represented the climax of his 14-year fight against the constitution of 1776.

For his services in the formation of the Federal government, in 1789 President Washington named him as an Associate Justice of the Supreme Court. He was chosen that same year as the first law professor at the College of Philadelphia. Two years hence, he began an official digest of the laws of Pennsylvania, a project he never completed.

Wilson did not achieve the success on the Supreme Court that his capabilities and experience promised. Indeed, during those years he was the object of much criticism and barely escaped impeachment. He tried to influence the enactment of legislation in Pennsylvania favorable to land speculators. Between 1792 and 1795, he also made huge but unwise land investments in western New York and Pennsylvania, and in Georgia. This did not stop him from conceiving a grandiose but ill-fated scheme involving vast sums of European capital, for the recruitment of European colonists and their settlement on western lands.

In 1797, to avoid arrest for debt, he moved from Philadelphia to Burlington, N.J. The next year, he arrived at Edenton, N.C., in a state of acute mental stress and was taken into the home of James Iredell, a fellow Supreme Court Justice. Wilson died there within a few months. Although first buried at Hayes Plantation near Edenton, his remains were later reinterred in Christ Churchyard at Philadelphia.

JOHN WITHERSPOON | NEW JERSEY

The son of a Calvinist minister, Witherspoon was born in 1723 at the village of Gifford, near Edinburgh, Scotland. He attended grammar school at the neighboring town of Haddington and won master of arts (1739) and divinity (1743) degrees from the University of Edinburgh. In 1743, the Haddington Presbytery licensed him to preach, and he was ordained two years later at Beith, where he occupied a pulpit until 1757. He then transferred to Paisley, not far from Glasgow.

In 1768, Witherspoon gave up his post at Paisley and accepted the presidency of the College of New Jersey, later Princeton, after two representatives of the college had visited him and finally, at the end of two years of effort, overcame the objections of his wife. He sailed to America with his family. The college bloomed under his direction. He increased the endowment, instituted new methods of instruction, and broadened and revitalized the curriculum. Continuing also as a minister and church leader, he patched up a major schism in the Presbyterian Church; stimulated its expansion, especially in the Middle Colonies; and worked closely with the Congregationalists.

The Revolution fanned Witherspoon's hatred of the English, which had originated in Scotland. By 1770, his students were openly demonstrating in favor of the patriot cause. In a commencement oration, he advocated resistance to the Crown, which became his favorite theme in sermons and essays. In 1774-1776, he represented his county in the New Jersey provincial assemblies and sat on local committees of correspondence. In 1776, he figured prominently in the agitations that led to the removal from office and imprisonment of the Royal Governor and then received an appointment to the Continental Congress.

In November 1776, when the British invaded New Jersey, he closed the College of New Jersey. The redcoats occupied the major building, Nassau Hall, burned the library, and committed other acts of destruction.

Witherspoon stayed in Congress until 1782. His main committee assignments dealt with military and foreign affairs. He also participated in the debates on the Articles of Confederation, aided in setting up the executive departments, and argued for financial stability. Meantime, in 1779, he had moved from the President's House at Princeton to Tusculum, a country home he earlier had built nearby. He left the Rev. Samuel S. Smith, the college vice president, in charge of the nearly defunct institution.

Witherspoon devoted most of his effort during the postwar years to rebuilding the college, which never fully recovered its prewar prosperity during his lifetime. In addition, during 1783-1789, he sat for two terms in the state legislature, attended the New Jersey (1787) convention that ratified the Federal Constitution, participated in the reorganization of the Presbyterian Church, and moderated its first general assembly (1789). Blind his last two years, he died in 1794, at age 71, at Tusculum. Witherspoon's remains rest in the President's Lot at Princeton Cemetery.

OLIVER WOLCOTT | CONNECTICUT

Wolcott, sired by Roger Wolcott, a leading Connecticut politician, was born in 1726 at Windsor (present South Windsor), Conn. In 1747, just graduated from Yale College at the top of his class, he began his military career. As a militia captain during King George's War (1740-1748), he accompanied an unsuccessful British expedition against the French in New France. Back home, he studied medicine with his brother before turning to law.

In 1751, when Litchfield County was organized, Wolcott moved to the town of Litchfield and immediately took over the first of a long string of county and state offices: county sheriff (1751-1771); member of the lower house (1764, 1767-1768, and 1770) and upper house (1771-1786) of the colonial and state legislatures; and probate (1772-1781) and county (1774-1778) judge. By 1774, he had risen to the rank of colonel in the militia.

The next spring, the legislature named him as a commissary for Connecticut troops, and in the summer the Continental Congress designated him as a commissioner of Indian affairs for the Northern Department. In that capacity he attended a conference that year with the Iroquois (Six Nations) at Albany, N.Y., that temporarily gained their neutrality in the war. Before the year was out, he aided in arbitrating land disputes between Pennsylvania and Connecticut and New York and Vermont.

Wolcott sat in Congress from 1775 until 1783 except for 1779. In June 1776, illness caused him to return to Connecticut. Absent at the time of the voting for independence in July and at the formal signing of the Declaration in August, he added his signature sometime after his return to Congress in October. Throughout his tour, Wolcott devoted portions of each year to militia duty, highlighted by participation as a brigadier general in the New York campaigns of 1776-1777 that culminated in the surrender of Gen. John Burgoyne in October 1777 at Saratoga (Schuylerville). During 1779, as a major general, Wolcott defended the Connecticut seacoast against the raids of William Tryon, Royal Governor of New York.

On the national level, Wolcott helped negotiate two Indian treaties: the Second Treaty of Fort Stanwix, N.Y. (1784), in which the Iroquois ceded to the United States some of their lands in New York and Pennsylvania; and another (1789) with the Wyandottes, who gave up their tract in the Western Reserve in present Ohio. On the state level, Wolcott continued his long period of service in the upper house of the legislature (ended 1786); enjoyed a lengthy stint as lieutenant governor (1787-1796); attended the convention (1788) that ratified the U.S. Constitution; and held the office of governor (1796-1797).

Still governor, Wolcott died at age 71 at East Windsor. His remains rest in the East Cemetery at Litchfield.

Wythe was born in 1726 on his father's plantation on the Back River in Elizabeth City County, Va., within the confines of present Hampton. He lost his parents at an early age and grew up under the guardianship of his older brother, Thomas.

Wythe's brother sent him to Prince George County to read law under an uncle. In 1746, at age 20, he joined the bar, moved to Spotsylvania County, and became associated with a lawyer there. In 1754, Lt. Gov. Robert Dinwiddie appointed him as acting colonial attorney general, a position he held for a few months and which likely required that he spend some time in Williamsburg. The next year, Wythe's brother died, and Wythe inherited his birthplace. He chose, however, to live in Williamsburg.

At Williamsburg, Wythe immersed himself in study of the classics and the law and achieved accreditation by the colonial Supreme Court. He served in the House of Burgesses (mid-1750s until 1775), first as delegate and after 1769 as clerk. In 1768, he held the mayorship of Williamsburg and the next year sat on the board of visitors of the College of William and Mary. He also had found time in 1762-1767 to train young Thomas Jefferson in the law. The two men, at first as mentor and pupil and later as political allies, maintained a lifetime friendship.

Wythe first exhibited Revolutionary leanings in 1764 when Parliament hinted to the Colonies that it might impose a Stamp Tax. By then an experienced legislator, he drafted for the House of Burgesses a remonstrance to Parliament so strident that his fellow legislators modified it before adoption. Wythe was one of the first to express the concept of separate nationhood for the Colonies within the British Empire.

Although elected to Congress in 1775-1776, Wythe exerted little influence there. He spent considerable time helping draft a state constitution and designing a state seal, and was not present at the formal signing of the Declaration in August 1776. Furthermore, within a few months, Wythe, Jefferson, and Edmund Pendleton undertook a three-year project to revise Virginia's legal code. In 1777, Wythe presided as speaker of the lower house of the legislature.

An appointment as one of the three judges of the newly created Virginia high court of chancery followed in 1778. Sitting on it for 28 years, during 13 of which he was the only chancellor, Wythe charted the course of Virginia jurisprudence. In conjunction with these duties, he was an ex officio member of the state Superior Court.

Wythe's real love was teaching. In 1779, Jefferson and other officials of the College of William and Mary created the first chair of law in a U.S. institution of higher learning and appointed Wythe to fill it. In that position, he educated America's earliest college-trained lawyers, among them John Marshall and James Monroe. To supplement his lectures, Wythe introduced the use of moot courts and legislatures, in which students could put their knowledge into actual practice. In 1787, he also demonstrated his love of the classics and literature by offering free a class in Latin, Greek, and English literature. That same year, he attended the U.S. Constitutional Convention but played an insignificant role and did not sign the Constitution. The following year, however, he was one of the Federalist leaders at the Virginia ratifying convention.

In 1791, the year after Wythe resigned his professorship, his chancery duties caused him to move to Richmond, the state capital. But he was reluctant to give up his teaching and opened a private law school.

In 1806, in his eighties, Wythe died at Richmond under mysterious circumstances—probably of poison administered by a grandnephew. Reflecting a lifelong aversion to slavery, Wythe emancipated his slaves in his will. His grave is in the yard of St. John's Episcopal Church at Richmond.

The Sons of Liberty yanking down the statue of King George III in New York, July 9, 1776. Color engraving by John McRae.

Reading the Declaration of Independence before George Washington's army at New York, July 9, 1776. Illustration by Howard Pyle.

In Congress, July 4, 1776

The unanimous Declaration of the thirteen united States of America

When in the Course of human events, it becomes necessary for one people to dissolve the political bands which have connected them with another, and to assume among the powers of the earth, the separate and equal station to which the Laws of Nature and of Nature's God entitle them, a decent respect to the opinions of mankind requires that they should declare the causes which impel them to the separation.

We hold these truths to be self-evident, that all men are created equal, that they are endowed by their Creator with certain unalienable Rights, that among these are Life, Liberty and the pursuit of Happiness.—— That to secure these rights, Governments are instituted among Men, deriving their just powers from the consent of the governed.—— That whenever any Form of Government becomes destructive of these ends, it is the Right of the People to alter or to abolish it, and to institute new Government, laying its foundation on such principles and organizing its powers in such form, as to them shall seem most likely to effect their Safety and Happiness. Prudence, indeed, will dictate that Governments long established should not be changed for light and transient causes; and accordingly all experience hath shewn, that mankind are more disposed to suffer, while evils are sufferable, than to right themselves by abolishing the forms to which they are accustomed. But when a long train of abuses and usurpations, pursuing invariably the same Object evinces a design to reduce them under absolute Despotism, it is their right, it is their duty, to throw off such Government, and to provide new Guards for their future security,—Such has been the patient sufferance of these Colonies; and such is now the necessity which constrains them to alter their former Systems of Government. The history of the present King of Great Britain is a history of repeated injuries and usurpations, all having in direct object the establishment of an absolute Tyranny over these States. To prove this, let Facts be submitted to a candid world.

He has refused his Assent to Laws, the most wholesome and necessary for the public good.

He has forbidden his Governors to pass Laws of immediate and pressing importance, unless suspended in their operation till his Assent should be obtained; and when so suspended, he has utterly neglected to attend to them.

He has refused to pass other Laws for the accommodation of large districts of people, unless those people would relinquish the right of Representation in the Legislature, a right inestimable to them and formidable to tyrants only.

He has called together legislative bodies at places unusual, uncomfortable, and distant from the depository of their public Records, for the sole purpose of fatiguing them into compliance with his measures.

He has dissolved Representative Houses repeatedly, for opposing with manly firmness his invasions on the rights of the people.

He has refused for a long time, after such dissolutions, to cause others to be elected; whereby the Legislative powers, incapable of Annihilation, have returned to the People at large for their exercise; the State remaining in the meantime exposed to all the dangers of invasion from without, and convulsions within.

He has endeavoured to prevent the population of these States; for that purpose obstructing the Laws for Naturalization of Foreigners; refusing to pass others to encourage their migrations hither, and raising the conditions of new Appropriation of Lands.

He has obstructed the Administration of Justice, by refusing his Assent to Laws for establishing Judiciary powers.

He has made Judges dependent on his Will alone, for the tenure of their offices, and the amount and payment of their salaries.

He has erected a multitude of New Offices, and sent hither swarms of Officers to harass our people, and eat out their substance.

He has kept among us, in times of peace, Standing Armies without the Consent of our legislatures.

He has affected to render the Military independent of and superior to the Civil power.

He has combined with others to subject us to a jurisdiction foreign to our constitution, and unacknowledged by our laws; giving his Assent to their Acts of pretended Legislation:

For Quartering large bodies of armed troops among us:

For protecting them, by a mock Trial, from punishment for any Murders which they should commit on the Inhabitants of these States:

For cutting off our Trade with all parts of the world:

For imposing Taxes on us without our Consent:

For depriving us in many cases, of the benefits of Trial by Jury:

For transporting us beyond Seas to be tried for pretended offences

For abolishing the free System of English Laws in a neighbouring Province, establishing therein an Arbitrary government, and enlarging its Boundaries so as to render it at once an example and fit instrument for introducing the same absolute rule into these Colonies:

For taking away our Charters, abolishing our most valuable Laws, and altering fundamentally the Forms of our Governments:

For suspending our own Legislatures and declaring themselves invested with power to legislate for us in all cases whatsoever.

He has abdicated Government here, by declaring us out of his Protection and waging War against us.

He has plundered our seas, ravaged our Coasts, burnt our towns, and destroyed the lives of our people.

He is at this time transporting large Armies of foreign Mercenaries to compleat the works of death, desolation and tyranny, already begun with circumstances of Cruelty & perfidy scarcely paralleled in the most barbarous ages, and totally unworthy the Head of a civilized nation.

He has constrained our fellow Citizens taken Captive on the high Seas to bear Arms against their Country, to become the executioners of their friends and Brethren, or to fall themselves by their Hands.

He has excited domestic insurrections amongst us, and has endeavoured to bring on the inhabitants of our frontiers, the merciless Indian Savages, whose known rule of warfare, is an undistinguished destruction of all ages, sexes and conditions.

In every stage of these Oppressions we have Petitioned for Redress in the most humble terms: our repeated Petitions have been answered only by repeated injury. A Prince, whose character is thus marked by every act which may define a Tyrant, is unfit to be the ruler of a free people.

Nor have We been wanting in attention to our British brethren. We have warned them from time to time of attempts by their legislature to extend an unwarrantable jurisdiction over us. We have reminded them of the circumstances of our emigration and settlement here. We have appealed to their native justice and magnanimity, and we have conjured them by the ties of our common kindred to disavow these usurpations, which, would inevitably interrupt our connections and correspondence. They too have been deaf to the voice of justice and of consanguinity. We must, therefore, acquiesce in the necessity, which denounces our Separation, and hold them, as we hold the rest of mankind, Enemies in War, in Peace Friends.

We, therefore, the Representatives of the united States of America, in General Congress, Assembled, appealing to the Supreme Judge of the world for the rectitude of our intentions, do, in the Name, and by Authority of the good People of these Colonies, solemnly publish and declare, That these United Colonies are, and of Right ought to be Free and Independent States; that they are Absolved from all Allegiance to the British Crown, and that all political connection between them and the State of Great Britain, is and ought to be totally dissolved; and that as Free and Independent States, they have full Power to levy War, conclude Peace, contract Alliances, establish Commerce, and to do all other Acts and Things which Independent States may of right do.

And for the support of this Declaration, with a firm reliance on the protection of divine Providence, we mutually pledge to each other our Lives, our Fortunes and our sacred Honor.

Thomas Jefferson reading his draft of the
Declaration to Benjamin Franklin.

HISTORY OF THE DOCUMENT

The best known of all the copies of the Declaration of Independence is the parchment copy, engrossed by Timothy Matlack. This one, signed by 56 Delegates of the Continental Congress on and after August 2, 1776, is displayed today in Exhibition Hall at the National Archives Building. Jefferson's final draft of the Declaration, known as the "rough draft," cumulatively bearing the corrections, amendments, and deletions of the drafting committee and of Congress as a whole, as well as Jefferson's marginal and textual notes, is preserved among the Jefferson Papers at the Library of Congress. The revised draft, adopted by the delegates on July 4, 1776, and signed only by John Hancock and Charles Thomson, president and secretary of the Continental Congress, is known as the broadside copy. It was sent to the printer and has never been located. Sixteen copies of the printed broadside have survived. In addition to the "rough draft," at least six other handwritten contemporary copies of the Declaration, one fragmentary, have survived and are in various archival collections. Five were made by Jefferson and one by John Adams.

The history of the parchment copy of the Declaration is fascinating. From 1776 until 1789, along with other important national papers, it was safeguarded by Secretary of Congress Thomson, who carried it with him as Congress, at first to escape British troops and later for other reasons, convened in various cities: Philadelphia, Baltimore, Lancaster, York, Princeton, Trenton, Annapolis, and New York.

When the Constitution took effect in 1789 and Thomson left office, he relinquished the Declaration to the newly created Department of State, which was under the temporary stewardship of Acting Secretary John Jay. The department's offices were in New York's old City Hall (Federal Hall). The next March, Thomas Jefferson became the first secretary of state and custodian of the instrument he had created. Later that year, Philadelphia became the seat of the Federal Government and the Declaration returned to its birthplace. There it remained for a decade, until 1800, when the Government moved to the new national capital of Washington.

Secretary of State John Marshall apparently at first stored the Declaration in his department's temporary offices in the old Treasury Building, at 15th Street and Pennsylvania Avenue NW, and possibly then at Seven Buildings, 19th Street and Pennsylvania Avenue NW. After a few months, likely in 1801, the document was transferred to the War Office Building at 17th Street and Pennsylvania Avenue NW, where the Department of State moved its offices. The Declaration remained there until the summer of 1814, during the War of 1812, when British troops invaded the capital. Shortly before they arrived, Secretary of State James Monroe packed the instrument and other state papers in linen sacks and sent them by wagon to a barn on the Virginia side of the Potomac two miles above Chain

Bridge for one night, and then to a clergyman's home in Leesburg, Va. Within a few weeks, after the British threat had subsided, the documents were brought back to Washington and probably temporarily kept in various structures because of the burning of the War Office Building by the British.

In 1820, the Department of State moved the Declaration to its headquarters at 15th Street and Pennsylvania Avenue NW. Stored for years in scroll fashion, the document had already been damaged by numerous unrollings, other handling, and frequent moves. In the period 1820-1823, the use of a "wet" copying process to produce a facsimile apparently divested the parchment of some of its ink, especially that of the signatures.

Subsequently, the Declaration remained relatively undisturbed until 1841, when Secretary of State Daniel Webster, concluding that it should be on public view, ordered that it be mounted, framed, and moved to the newly constructed Patent Office, in the block bounded by Seventh, Ninth, F, and G Streets NW. The Patent Office was then part of the Department of State. Placed beside George Washington's commission as commander in chief of the Continental Army in a large frame on a wall of the second floor hall opposite a window, for 35 years the Declaration endured exposure to glare, summer heat, and winter cold. The text retained its legibility, but the parchment faded and yellowed, cracked, and warped. Many of the signatures had faded, some becoming blurred or almost invisible.

The Federal Government in 1876 lent the Declaration to the city of Philadelphia, site of the national Centennial Exposition. On July 4, Richard Henry Lee, grandson of the signer, read it publicly. It was then exhibited in a fireproof safe behind a plate glass window and seen by more people than ever before. Philadelphians, deploring its condition, fought to retain it and only reluctantly returned it to Washington. Heeding the outcry of those who had viewed the timeworn parchment, a government commission studied the possibility of restoration and in time concluded that such an attempt might be damaging.

Meantime, in 1877, as a safeguard the Declaration was moved from the Patent Office to a more fire-resistant building at 17th Street and Pennsylvania Avenue NW shared by the State, War, and Navy Departments. It had narrowly escaped destruction, for only a few months later fire gutted the Patent Office. Finally, in 1894, for protection from the light, State Department officials sealed the 118-year-old sheet between two glass plates and locked it in a safe in the basement. There it lay, except for rare occasions, in darkness and unobserved for more than a quarter of a century.

In 1921, the Department of State, responding to the recommendation of a special commission, relinquished custodianship of the Declaration to the Library of Congress. The transfer was made personally by Herbert Putnam, the librarian, using a library mail truck, a Model T Ford. At first he kept the document in his office. In 1924, however, he placed it together with the Constitution on public exhibition in a bronze and marble shrine on the second floor. At this time, the Declaration was encased between heavy glass panes specially treated to keep out harmful rays of light.

The Declaration and the Constitution remained there until the outbreak of World War II. On December 26, 1941, just 19 days after the Japanese attack on Pearl Harbor, they left Washington under heavy guard by train en route to Fort Knox, Ky., where they arrived the following day. Specialists took advantage of the opportunity and cleaned and restored the Declaration to the maximum degree. In 1944, both it and the Constitution were taken back to the Library of Congress. They remained there until 1952, at which time a tank under military escort carried them to Washington's National Archives Building, repository of the nation's permanent records, which are under the jurisdiction of the National Archives and Records Service of the U.S. General Services Administration.

Still enshrined there today, along with thousands of other priceless national records, is the parchment copy of the Declaration. The massive bronze doors at the Constitution Avenue entrance to the building lead to the circular Exhibition Hall. At its rear center stands a marble shrine containing the Declaration of Independence, the Constitution, and the Bill of Rights. They are sealed in helium-filled bronze and glass cases, screened from harmful light rays by special filters, and can be lowered within seconds into a large fireproof, shockproof, and bombproof vault.

The hall also features a "Formation of the Union" exhibit, a collection of documents illustrating the evolution of the U.S. Government from 1774 until 1791. They include the Articles of Association (1774), the Articles of Confederation (1777), the Treaty of Paris (1783), and Washington's inaugural address (1789). Above the exhibits are two murals. In one, Jefferson is presenting the Declaration to John Hancock, president of the Continental Congress; in the other, James Madison is submitting the Constitution to George Washington, president of the Constitutional Convention.

IMAGE CREDITS

Portraits of the Signers listed by page

19 John Adams by Charles Willson Peale, from life, c. 1791-1794 - INHP

21 Samuel Adams by Nahum Ball Onthank, after John Singleton Copely, c. 1873 - INHP

24 Josiah Bartlett by Caroline Weeks, after John Trumbull, c. 1871 - INHP

25 Carter Braxton (assumed) likeness, after a miniature by an unidentified artist

26 Charles Carroll by Charles Willson Peale, after Rembrandt Peale, c. 1823 - INHP

28 Samuel Chase by Charles Willson Peale, after Charles Willson Peale, c. 1819 - INHP

29 Abraham Clark by James Read Lambdin, after John Trumbull, c. 1872 - INHP

31 George Clymer by Edward Marchant, after Charles Willson Peale, c. 1872 - INHP

32 William Ellery by James Read Lambdin, after John Trumbull, 1872 - INHP

33 William Floyd by Ralph Earl, from life, c. 1793 - INHP

34 Benjamin Franklin by David Rent Etter, after Charles Willson Peale, after David Martin, 1835 - INHP

37 Elbridge Gerry by James Bogle, after John Vanderlyn, 1861 - INHP

39 Button Gwinnett, artist and date unknown - LOC

40 Lyman Hall, artist and date unknown - LOC

44 John Hancock by Samuel Finley Breese Morse, after John Singleton Copley, c. 1816 - INHP

46 Benjamin Harrison by James Read Lambdin, after John Trumbull, 1873 - INHP

47 John Hart by Herman F. Deigendisch, after Henry Bryan Hall, 1895 - INHP

48 Joseph Hewes by Georges D'Almaine, after Charles Willson Peale, 1875 - INHP

49 Thomas Heyward, Jr., by Charles Fraser, after Jeremiah Theus, c. 1825-1850 - INHP

51 William Hooper by James Read Lambdin, after John Trumbull, 1873 - INHP

52 Stephen Hopkins (assumed) likeness by John Hagen, 1999, Brown University Portrait Collection

54 Francis Hopkinson by an unidentified artist, possibly Charles Willson Peale or Samuel F. Dubois, after Robert Edge Pine, before 1854 - INHP

55 Samuel Huntington by Charles Willson Peale, from life, 1783 - INHP

56 Thomas Jefferson by Charles Willson Peale, from life, 1791-1792 - INHP

59 Francis Lightfoot Lee by unknown artist, courtesy of The Menokin Foundation

60 Richard Henry Lee by Charles Willson Peale from life, c. 1785 - INHP

62 Francis Lewis reproduction of oil painting by Albert Rosenthal, after engraving at Independence Hall, date unknown - LOC

63 Philip Livingston oil on canvas portrait 1783 by Pompeo-Girolamo Batoni (1708-1787), Marriner S. Eccles Collection of Masterworks, from the permanent collection of the Utah Museum of Fine Arts

65 Thomas Lynch, Jr., by Anna Lea Merritt, after James Barton Longacre engraving from an unknown miniature, 1875 - INHP

68 Thomas McKean by Charles Willson Peale from life, 1797 - INHP

70 Arthur Middleton by Philip Fisbourne Wharton, after Benjamin West, c. 1872 - INHP

71 Lewis Morris by Charles Noel Flagg, after John Trumbull, c. 1873 - INHP

72 Robert Morris by Charles Willson Peale, from life, c. 1872 - INHP

74 John Morton by Pierre Eugene DuSimitier, c. 1765, courtesy of the R.W. Norton Art Gallery, Shreveport, La.

75 Thomas Nelson, Jr., by William Ludlow Sheppard, after Mason Chamberlain, c. 1876 - INHP

76 William Paca by Francis Blackwell Mayer, after Charles Willson Peale, c. 1874 - INHP

78 Robert Treat Paine by Richard Morrell Staigg, after Edward Savage, c. 1876 - INHP

79 John Penn, possibly from engraving by H.B. Hall - LOC

80 George Read by Thomas Sully, after Robert Edge Pine, c. 1860 - INHP

82 Caesar Rodney by Charles Balthazar Julien Fevret de Saint-Mémin, 1800 - LOC

83 George Ross by Philip Fisbourne Wharton, after Benjamin West, c. 1873 - INHP

84 Benjamin Rush by Charles Willson Peale, after Thomas Sully, 1818 - INHP

86 Edward Rutledge by Philip Fisbourne Wharton, after James Earl, c. 1873 - INHP

88 Roger Sherman by Thomas Hicks, after Ralph Earl, c. 1866 - INHP

89 James Smith by unknown American artist, c. 1760, courtesy of the R.W. Norton Art Gallery, Shreveport, La.

90 Richard Stockton by George Washington Conarroe, after a painting attributed to John Wollaston, c. 1876 - INHP

91 Thomas Stone by Francis Blackwell Mayer, after John Beale Bordley after Robert Edge Pine, 1874 - INHP

92 George Taylor photo of sketch, artist and date unknown - LOC

93 Matthew Thornton oil on canvas by Nahum Ball Onthank, c. 1870, courtesy of The New Hampshire Historical Society

95 George Walton by Samuel Bell Waugh, after Charles Willson Peale, c. 1874 - INHP

96 William Whipple by Ulysses D. Tenney, 1888, courtesy of the Moffatt-Ladd House and Garden, Portsmouth, N.H.

97 William Williams by James J. Sawyer, after John Trumbull, 1873 - INHP

98 James Wilson by Philip Fisbourne Wharton, after the James Barton Longacre engraving from a painting by Jean Pierre Henri Elouis, 1873 - INHP

101 John Witherspoon by Charles Willson Peale, after Charles Willson Peale, 1783-1784 - INHP

102 Oliver Wolcott by James Read Lambdin, after Ralph Earl, 1873 - INHP

103 George Wythe by John Ferguson Weir, after John Trumbull, 1876 - INHP

INHP – Independence National Historical Park, Philadelphia, PA
LOC - Library of Congress

Cover image – The Signing of the Declaration of Independence by John Trumbull, Bridgeman Art Library

Images on pages 4, 42, 43, 64, 66, 74 courtesy of Independence NHP.

Images on pages 1, 2, 6, 7, 8, 9, 10, 11, 13, 18, 58, 70 from the Bridgeman Art Library.

Images on pages 3, 15, 16, 17, 24, 31, 41, 46, 77, 105, 106, 110, 116 from the Granger Collection.

Authors Robert G. Ferris and Richard E. Morris are former historians with the National Park Service.

Design by Therese Cruse.

Published by Eastern National, copyright 2014.

ISBN 978-1-59091-159-4

Eastern National provides quality educational products and services to the visitors to America's national parks and other public trusts.
Visit us at www.eParks.com

For more information on our national parks, visit www.nps.gov

IN CONGRESS, JULY 4, 1776

The unanimous Declaration of the thirteen united States of America.

When in the Course of human events, it becomes necessary for one people to dissolve the political bands which have connected them with another, and to assume among the powers of the earth, the separate and equal station to which the Laws of Nature and of Nature's God entitle them, a decent respect to the opinions of mankind requires that they should declare the causes which impel them to the separation.

We hold these truths to be self-evident, that all men are created equal, that they are endowed by their Creator with certain unalienable Rights, that among these are Life, Liberty and the pursuit of Happiness. — That to secure these rights, Governments are instituted among Men, deriving their just powers from the consent of the governed, — That whenever any Form of Government becomes destructive of these ends, it is the Right of the People to alter or to abolish it, and to institute new Government, laying its foundation on such principles and organizing its powers in such form, as to them shall seem most likely to effect their Safety and Happiness. Prudence, indeed, will dictate that Governments long established should not be changed for light and transient causes; and accordingly all experience hath shewn, that mankind are more disposed to suffer, while evils are sufferable, than to right themselves by abolishing the forms to which they are accustomed. But when a long train of abuses and usurpations, pursuing invariably the same Object evinces a design to reduce them under absolute Despotism, it is their right, it is their duty, to throw off such Government, and to provide new Guards for their future security. — Such has been the patient sufferance of these Colonies; and such is now the necessity which constrains them to alter their former Systems of Government. The history of the present King of Great Britain is a history of repeated injuries and usurpations, all having in direct object the establishment of an absolute Tyranny over these States. To prove this, let Facts be submitted to a candid world.

He has refused his Assent to Laws, the most wholesome and necessary for the public good.

He has forbidden his Governors to pass Laws of immediate and pressing importance, unless suspended in their operation till his Assent should be obtained; and when so suspended, he has utterly neglected to attend to them.

He has refused to pass other Laws for the accommodation of large districts of people, unless those people would relinquish the right of Representation in the Legislature, a right inestimable to them and formidable to tyrants only.

He has called together legislative bodies at places unusual, uncomfortable, and distant from the depository of their public Records, for the sole purpose of fatiguing them into compliance with his measures.

He has dissolved Representative Houses repeatedly, for opposing with manly firmness his invasions on the rights of the people.

He has refused for a long time, after such dissolutions, to cause others to be elected; whereby the Legislative powers, incapable of Annihilation, have returned to the People at large for their exercise; the State remaining in the mean time exposed to all the dangers of invasion from without, and convulsions within.

He has endeavoured to prevent the population of these States; for that purpose obstructing the Laws for Naturalization of Foreigners; refusing to pass others to encourage their migrations hither, and raising the conditions of new Appropriations of Lands.

He has obstructed the Administration of Justice, by refusing his Assent to Laws for establishing Judiciary powers.

He has made Judges dependent on his Will alone, for the tenure of their offices, and the amount and payment of their salaries.

He has erected a multitude of New Offices, and sent hither swarms of Officers to harrass our people, and eat out their substance.

He has kept among us, in times of peace, Standing Armies without the Consent of our legislatures.

He has affected to render the Military independent of and superior to the Civil power.

He has combined with others to subject us to a jurisdiction foreign to our constitution, and unacknowledged by our laws; giving his Assent to their Acts of pretended Legislation:

For Quartering large bodies of armed troops among us: — For protecting them, by a mock Trial, from punishment for any Murders which they should commit on the Inhabitants of these States: — For cutting off our Trade with all parts of the world: — For imposing Taxes on us without our Consent: — For depriving us in many cases, of the benefits of Trial by jury: — For transporting us beyond Seas to be tried for pretended offences: — For abolishing the free System of English Laws in a neighbouring Province, establishing therein an Arbitrary government, and enlarging its Boundaries so as to render it at once an example and fit instrument for introducing the same absolute rule into these Colonies: — For taking away our Charters, abolishing our most valuable Laws, and altering fundamentally the Forms of our Governments: — For suspending our own Legislatures, and declaring themselves invested with power to legislate for us in all cases whatsoever.

He has abdicated Government here, by declaring us out of his Protection and waging War against us.

He has plundered our seas, ravaged our Coasts, burnt our towns, and destroyed the lives of our people.

He is at this time transporting large Armies of foreign Mercenaries to compleat the works of death, desolation and tyranny, already begun with circumstances of Cruelty & perfidy scarcely paralleled in the most barbarous ages, and totally unworthy the Head of a civilized nation.

He has constrained our fellow Citizens taken Captive on the high Seas to bear Arms against their Country, to become the executioners of their friends and Brethren, or to fall themselves by their Hands.

He has excited domestic insurrections amongst us, and has endeavoured to bring on the inhabitants of our frontiers, the merciless Indian Savages, whose known rule of warfare, is an undistinguished destruction of all ages, sexes and conditions.

In every stage of these Oppressions We have Petitioned for Redress in the most humble terms: Our repeated Petitions have been answered only by repeated injury. A Prince whose character is thus marked by every act which may define a Tyrant, is unfit to be the ruler of a free people.

Nor have We been wanting in attentions to our British brethren. We have warned them from time to time of attempts by their legislature to extend an unwarrantable jurisdiction over us. We have reminded them of the circumstances of our emigration and settlement here. We have appealed to their native justice and magnanimity, and we have conjured them by the ties of our common kindred to disavow these usurpations, which, would inevitably interrupt our connections and correspondence. They too have been deaf to the voice of justice and of consanguinity. We must, therefore, acquiesce in the necessity, which denounces our Separation, and hold them, as we hold the rest of mankind, Enemies in War, in Peace Friends.

We, therefore, the Representatives of the united States of America, in General Congress, Assembled, appealing to the Supreme Judge of the world for the rectitude of our intentions, do, in the Name, and by Authority of the good People of these Colonies, solemnly publish and declare, That these United Colonies are, and of Right ought to be Free and Independent States; that they are Absolved from all Allegiance to the British Crown, and that all political connection between them and the State of Great Britain, is and ought to be totally dissolved; and that as Free and Independent States, they have full Power to levy War, conclude Peace, contract Alliances, establish Commerce, and to do all other Acts and Things which Independent States may of right do. And for the support of this Declaration, with a firm reliance on the protection of divine Providence, we mutually pledge to each other our Lives, our Fortunes and our sacred Honor.

John Hancock

Button Gwinnett
Lyman Hall
Geo Walton

Wm Hooper
Joseph Hewes
John Penn

Edward Rutledge

Thos Heyward Junr.
Thomas Lynch Junr.
Arthur Middleton

Samuel Chase
Wm Paca
Thos Stone
Charles Carroll of Carrollton

George Wythe
Richard Henry Lee
Th Jefferson
Benja Harrison
Thos Nelson jr.
Francis Lightfoot Lee
Carter Braxton

Robt Morris
Benjamin Rush
Benja Franklin
John Morton
Geo Clymer
Jas Smith
Geo Taylor
James Wilson
Geo Ross
Caesar Rodney
Geo Read
Tho M:Kean

Wm Floyd
Phil. Livingston
Frans Lewis
Lewis Morris

Richd Stockton
Jno Witherspoon
Fras Hopkinson
John Hart
Abra Clark

Josiah Bartlett
Wm Whipple
Saml Adams
John Adams
Robt Treat Paine
Elbridge Gerry
Step Hopkins
William Ellery
Roger Sherman
Saml Huntington
Wm Williams
Oliver Wolcott
Matthew Thornton